"I just finished reading Brian B *Executive: Maximize Your Bran* on Brian's years of experienc company, Media Connect Partn…, vant to executives, social media personnel, or any company in need of a social media strategy. The book emphasizes strategy and results, and uses real world examples to illustrate each concept. I've had the pleasure of working with Brian; and he is truly one of the most enthusiastic, capable people I have ever met. He always delivers and so does this book. I came away with a renewed understanding of the power of social media to deliver effective and measurable results.

Tim Archer, Grammy Award-winning recording artist,
and president, Tim Archer Music

"This book is a great resource for any organization, from those just starting to dabble in social media to brands that are already deeply immersed in the world of Facebook and Twitter. Brian has garnered great success for many companies through social media— and he can prove it. Measurable success has eluded many 'social media experts,' but Brian has been able to quantify a win beyond rattling off how many friends and followers your brand has."

Jeremy C. Burton, APR, senior director, university
relations and communications, Oral Roberts University

"I've been working in media for many years. As the CEO of INSP, I know the importance of social media and connecting with others. It's about relationships. In his new book, *Social Media for the Executive,* Brian clearly outlines what executives need to know to utilize social media effectively. After reading this book, you'll want to execute what you've learned immediately—or direct your marketing team to do so!"

David Cerullo, president and CEO, Inspiration Networks

"Brian has killer passion for social media, but his passion for helping his clients learn, stay on top, and be successful is even stronger. It's why this book's simple and direct information will cut through the normally overwhelming information and questions about social media, and put your company at the top of the search."

Kathleen Cooke, Co-founder/VP, Cooke Pictures,
Burbank, California

"Brian is one of the most gifted and efficacious communicators in the social media arena. His generosity of spirit in this new book shows why he is such a success. This is a great read for any executive trying to master social media and turn it into a productive business tool."

Wendy Grisham, publisher and VP, Jericho Books

"The right book at the right time! With much needed clarity, Brian Boyd delivers a challenging and fresh look at the power of Social Media for us executives. As a client, I can assure you that Brian practices what he preaches. Where social media can sometimes bring rapid change and even intimidation, the team at Media Connect Partners provides genuine strategy, support, and ROI for your business."

Rex Hamilton, founder and executive director,
HopeWorks, Seattle, Washington

"In a digital world teeming with so-called social media 'experts,' it's refreshing to get proven advice from a true social media professional like Brian Boyd. Boyd has a proven track record of social success, and his new book will certainly give you something to tweet about. For brands who are committed to integrating social media into their marketing mix, or for those brands who need to get off high-center when it comes to social engagement, this book is a must read."

Johnie Hampton, president and CEO, Hampton Creative

"Using examples and anecdotes that read like breezy conversation, Brian Boyd's *Social Media for the Executive* demonstrates how a company can 'communicate, connect, and convert' using this century's most dynamic business tool. You can't afford to be invisible. Learn from someone on the front lines of the social media revolution."

Nancy Hermann, director of marketing,
Tulsa Performing Arts Center

"Brian is one of us 'older folks' who actually understand what our kids take for granted! His fresh approach to social media helps it make sense to those of us who want tangible, financial results, not just a bunch of 'friends.' If you are still holding out, thinking you can skip the whole social media thing, read this book and reconsider quickly!"

John McB. Hodgson, MD, managing partner,
BioInfo Accelerator Fund, professor of medicine,
interventional cardiologist, chairman of the board,
Hope Educational Foundation (www.hopeeducation.org)

"Is social media worth it? Drilled to the core, that is what I—and every executive—want to ask. Brian has written a thought-leading book that vividly explains why every brand needs to commit to excellence in their social media presence in order to remain relevant. This book is an insightful journey from a theoretical overview of social media concepts to a succinct explanation of what you need to know about the details of social media as an executive. Social media is about relationships that convert. This book will prove it."

Rob Hoskins, president, OneHope, Inc.

"Throughout history, every so often the world changes. The Roman road network forever changed the way people traveled. The Wright brothers' invention went on to allow millions to take to the skies. The atomic bomb forever changed the way wars are fought. Social media has changed the way we communicate, evaluate, contribute, and consume. Who would have thought that a website developed in a dorm room by a certain man named Zuckerberg would change the world we live in so drastically?

"Every new invention demands a new type of champion – someone who understands the times and technologies and has the ability to lead others into this brave new world. I believe Brian Boyd is such a champion. Through this book, he leads all those who would follow into a new age of innovation, seamless communication, and unimagined influence!"

Jurie Kreil, Doxa Deo, Pretoria, South Africa

"WHY and HOW to monetize social media is an art, and Brian Boyd is the master artist. I loved this book as a handbook and motivator for learning more and earning more via social media. It's also a really fun read!"

Lynette Lewis, speaker, consultant,
author of *Climbing the Ladder in Stilettos*

"If you are involved in leadership, understanding the times and burgeoning communication technologies are essential. *Social Media for the Executive* by Brian Boyd gives a clear picture of the landscape of relationship gathering in this present day. Brian is a hero to those of us who must find ways to make our businesses work with measurable results.

"The social media landscape is the next place where the intersection of commerce and communication must reside and thrive. I recommend this book to all who value the art of triumph and victory, both financial and relational, in this new era of communication."

Ossie Mills, executive vice president,
Oral Roberts University

"Business as usual is dead. Social media is alive and an absolute must in order to maximize your possibilities, get your message out, and communicate with the largest number of people in the least amount of time. Brian Boyd has a wealth of knowledge on this subject that he generously and clearly shares in his new book, *Social Media for the Executive*. I loved it! It was eye-opening and life-changing for me. I couldn't put it down."

Stormie Omartian, best-selling author
(more than 23 million books sold)

"Brian Boyd offers a comprehensive, scalable, and secure reference in this book to help individuals and enterprises respond quickly, efficiently, and accurately with their audience and customers. This book will convince you that social media is not a passing fad or novelty, but an entirely new and essential way of doing business. It really just makes so much sense!"

Alan Platt, leader Doxa Deo/The City Changers Movement,
author of *We Start at Finish*

"I had the opportunity to meet Brian and his lovely wife Fran several years ago as our company struggled to find its footing in a rapidly evolving social media driven world that we didn't entirely understand. Brian and his team know their stuff! They were able to connect the dots for me as CEO and delivered on all that they promised."

Chris Reading, president/CEO, U.S. Physical Therapy, Inc.

"Brian Boyd helped me understand the value of engagement. In a world where everyone seems to have something to say, he taught me a better approach than just throwing marketing mud on a wall and hoping it sticks. Brian showed me a powerful new way to develop loyal customers and repeat business.

"Brian encouraged me to connect with customers and prospects alike by listening to and engaging with them through social media. In doing so, our executive team gained access to thought leaders throughout the world and have developed newfound influence as their voices now rise above the chatter.

"The must-read insights and strategies found in *Social Media for the Executive: Maximize Your Brand and Monetize Your Business* are the same ones Brian used to help me unlock the power of engagement. Through straight talk and loads of examples, Brian guides readers with practical ways to become better social media participants. I highly recommend this book and expect that it will do for others what it has done for me and my business."

Dan Roberts, entrepreneur, president, founder,
Trak-1 and HireCall

"Brian Boyd does a great job of telling the world why social media is no longer a choice, but simply a part of doing business in today's marketplace. This easy-to-read book will transform your thinking about social media as a passing fad to recognizing it is an essential business outreach, communication, networking, and conversation tool. The Social Revolution is here to stay, and Brian Boyd explains how you can become a part of it. This book is a must read for today's businessperson, whether you have no interest in social media or are moderately involved in it. Today's businesses must know how to do social, and Brian Boyd will help them do social right."

Nancy Lynn Roberts, Esq., business owner,
compliance officer, Trak-1, author

"When I needed to take my brand's social media presence to the next level, I brought in Brian and his team. They spent time with us to learn about our business and helped us to better articulate our goals for our foray into this new space. They emphasized authenticity and honesty with our fans and followers. And they weren't just satisfied posting and tweeting; they genuinely saw the potential of social media to be so much more engaging and interactive. They proposed innovative combinations of technologies to bring in new audiences and more closely connect us with existing members. They were genuinely sold on the value of social media when many supposed gurus were still on the fence about its long-term value for businesses. Brian and his team don't just spout the appropriate buzzwords, they live and breathe social media and really 'walk the walk.' To borrow a phrase from Carly Simon, 'Nobody does it better.'"

Lisa Schnettler, IT director, New York, New York

"Brian Boyd knows of what he speaks. And in his book, *Social Media for the Executive: Maximize Your Brand and Monetize your Business*, he speaks in terms that are easy to comprehend whether or not you're an executive. The concepts presented are solid in their foundation and reasoning. One doesn't need to be a social media expert to understand the book's language and, once started, the anecdotes along with the subject matter compel the reader to finish. Brian's recommendations have made a huge difference in the reach of our business."

John E. Scott, director, Tulsa Performing Arts Center

"It is my privilege to recommend Brian Boyd and his new book, *Social Media for the Executive: Maximize Your Brand and Monetize Your Business*. At Food for the Hungry, Brian has provided a breadth of wisdom and insight for our social media strategy and enhanced our presence in this space. When Brian speaks...we listen. He is the leader in social media execution for charities and executives. This is a must read!"

Timothy Smith, chief development officer,
Food for the Hungry

"In the fitness industry, where the goal is to help people change their lives, social media is a powerful tool. It allows you to build relationships with clients by connecting outside of training sessions—the time when people often need the most support and motivation. Telling and sharing success stories through social media will motivate current clients and inspire new ones to grow your business."

Michele Stanten, ACE-certified fitness instructor,
author of *Walk Off Weight*

"Brian is one of the most enthusiastic and strategic champions of social media with whom I've collaborated. His commitment to getting beyond the buzzwords and snake oil, and diving into what make digital tools meaningful and critical to the bottom line, can't be understated. I'm excited for *Social Media for the Executive!*"

Deanna Zandt, co-founder/partner, Lux Digital;
author, *Share This! How You Will Change the World with Social Networking*

SOCIAL MEDIA
—————FOR THE—————
EXECUTIVE

MAXIMIZE YOUR BRAND AND MONETIZE YOUR BUSINESS

BY

BRIAN E. BOYD, SR.

Social Media for the Executive:
Maximize Your Brand and Monetize Your Business
© 2013 by Brian Boyd

Published by One Seed Press
7131 Riverside Parkway
Tulsa, OK 74136
918-933-5959

All rights reserved. No part of this book may be reproduced or transmitted in any form or by any means, electronic or mechanical, including photocopying and recording, or by any information storage and retrieval system, without permission in writing from the author.

ISBN: 978-1-939250-08-7
Library of Congress Control Number: 2013941121

Printed in Canada

Dedication

This book is dedicated to three people who have had a major impact on who I am today.

Fran (@franpaceboyd)—You are the most amazing wife and life partner anyone could ask for. I'm so lucky to have you in my life. As you know, we'd still be "you know where" if you hadn't kicked me in the butt all those years ago and pushed me along. After 9/11, you were the one who inspired me to reboot my career while we were displaced and living in that hotel room. You are an awesome mom to @sarahboyd and @brianboydjr and we are all so fortunate to have you in our lives. I love you.

Grandpa Anderson—You were an awesome man of God and you talked for a living. Up until the day you passed you hustled, working and teaching. Two character traits you gave me which I'll always cherish: 1) Being on time to everything, and 2) Honesty and integrity in communication. You meant the world to me.

Dad—You have been in sales your whole life. When I was five years old, I rode with you over the Golden Gate Bridge to sell exercise equipment. I long thought that sales trait would do me no good, but look at me now—I "sell" myself and my passion every day. I never saw that coming. Thank you for all you taught me.

Contents

Acknowledgments..15

Foreword..17

Chapter 1   Social Media:
What It Is and Why You Need It......................19

Chapter 2   Three C's of Social Media Success..................31

Chapter 3   Know Your Goals...41

Chapter 4   Find Your Brand's Social Media Fit...................51

Chapter 5   Content Is King...61

Chapter 6   Influence: Why You Need It
and How to Get It...79

Chapter 7   Building the Relationship
(Measuring your ROR—
Return on Relationship)...................................91

Chapter 8   Creating a Solid Social Media Strategy.........105

Chapter 9   Maintaining Your Social Media Edge
(Keep an Eye on the Periphery)......................119

Epilogue..127

Acknowledgments

I would like to express my gratitude to the many people who supported me through this venture—my first book.

Thanks to Sarah (@sarahboyd) and Brian Jr. (@brianboydjr). You are the best kids any dad could have. Brian, I'll never forget how you kept asking me, "What chapter are you on, Dad?"—I needed that! Sarah—you've graduated college cum laude and you're a business maven. Mom and I are blessed and I love you both so much.

Mom, thank you for being mom! Love you!!

I would like to thank the team at One Seed Press for their help, especially Dan and Nancy Roberts, whose serial entrepreneurism created the company who pushed me along.

Thanks to Jim Kochenburger, my editor. Jim—you did a phenomenal job of 1) Pushing me when I was crazy busy flying around the world, 2) Somehow turning my ideas into words and clear communication, and 3) Bringing me to the finish line.

Thanks to the team at MCP. You are the smart ones. Your ability to keep the business running helped give me the time to complete this book. You rock.

I'd have to give a special thanks to the Communication Arts Department at Oral Roberts University—especially my Oral Communications teacher(s). As I look back at what I learned at @OralRobertsU in 1984, I know it was a class that influenced my career and gave me courage to speak in front of crowds. Thanks.

Last and not least: Friends and family who've given me encouraging words during this journey—thank you! It's been fun to share the process of this book on social media and see so many of you like, follow, and share. Keep sharing.

Foreword

I've known Brian Boyd since he was a college student and worked for me, running camera at the on-campus television studio. From the beginning, two things always stood out about him. First—he was relentlessly positive. No matter what happened and no matter the crisis, Brian refused to panic and always focused on how he could contribute to finding a solution. Second, he was always growing. I've rarely met anyone with such a strong curiosity or desire to expand his thinking.

Over the years, those two traits have taken Brian from a college media job to running an incredibly influential social media company: Media Connect Partners. Because he is so focused on growth, he saw the rise of social media long before most. Today, when everyone with Twitter or Facebook accounts think they're social media "experts," I'm reminded of the handful of innovators like Brian who recognized the phenomenon when most of us thought it was for teenagers at parties.

As a result, back when most people were posting Facebook pictures of their taco platter at the Mexican restaurant, or using Twitter to let the world know they were at Starbucks, Brian recognized that a solid social media strategy could change perceptions, impact business, and shift culture.

Set this book down at your peril. *Social Media for the Executive* is the culmination of years of working with both business leaders and nonprofit organizations on how to strategically use today's social media platforms to share their story and vision with the world. It will answer your questions about engaging with social media, tracking its return on investment, and how your organization should think about the future.

By the time you read this book, specific platforms like Twitter, Facebook, Pinterest, and others may have gone the way of

MySpace. *But make no mistake—social media is here to stay.* Your ability to engage socially with customers, donors, and other relationships will mean more and more as time goes by. This is your chance to understand that world. It's your chance to discover how connectivity happens. *And perhaps most of all, it's your chance to share your visions, dreams, and ideas with the world.*

> Phil Cooke, Ph.D.
> @PhilCooke
>
> Filmmaker, media consultant, and author of *Unique: Telling Your Story in the Age of Brands and Social Media*

CHAPTER 1

Social Media:
What It Is and Why You Need It

> "A brand is no longer what we tell the consumer it is—
> it is what consumers tell each other it is."
>
> —Scott Cook

Prevention, a health magazine based in New York, pushes out content to social media to find out what readers want to read about concerning diet, health, exercise, or politics, and receive a mother lode of rich feedback to drive their editorial content.

The *Teen Choice Awards Tour* reallocates significant resources from traditional marketing mediums to social media, and as a result, sees tremendous results and record-breaking ticket sales for their tour events.

Within ninety days of applying a comprehensive social media strategy with Media Connect Partners (MCP), the global nonprofit, Food for the Hungry, gets 36 percent more unique visitors to its website, 25 percent more likes and follows to their social media presence, and a 23 percent retweet rate on Twitter.

> Social media is not a passing fad or novelty,
> but an entirely new way of doing business.

Social media is not a passing fad or novelty, but an entirely new way of doing business. Brands that will survive and thrive from now on are those with C-level executives that understand the incredible opportunity new media offers them and commit to excellence in managing their social media presence. Whether you like social media or not, feel comfortable with it or not, engage in it or not, you cannot afford to ignore it because it is likely many of your competitors are using it effectively. In fact, if you do not use it, you run the risk of your business becoming invisible to friends and fans, as well as current and potential customers or clients. For your business to stand out and succeed, you have to put a primary focus on the social media space, go in big (halfway will not do), and do it better than most, right from the start.

> Social media is the opportunity for you and your brand to connect and build relationships.
>
> Social media is your opportunity to reach a massive number of people with transparency, honesty, and integrity.
>
> Social media is your chance to give access to your brand and your product to everybody—to level the playing field.

Why Social Media?

Social media is the opportunity for you and your brand to connect and build relationships. It goes far beyond TV and the old forms of one-way media. It is interactive, not only allowing you to deliver a message, but to garner a response. It provides you with an unprecedented opportunity to show the true you (corporately or personally) to your friends, family, potential customers, and business partners, whether B-to-B (business-to-business) or B-to-C (business-to-consumer). Social media is your opportunity to reach a massive number of people with transparency, honesty, and integrity. It is not necessarily the opportunity for you to sell something—not at first (though that will come)—but it is a unique opportunity to establish your image and build relationships which can build lists, or bring you leads, conversions, sales, and whatever else is important to you as a company.

Social media is your chance to give access to your brand and your product to everybody—to level the playing field. This was the promise of websites back in 1994 and 1995 when they started coming along. Back then, you could go to the websites for Microsoft, McDonald's, Intel, or Domino's and no matter where you were in the country or world, gain access that was impossible even a year or two before. Suddenly, consumers and clients had the ability to "talk" to any company directly. Fast forward to now and we have taken another huge leap forward. Now every brand, every company, every organization has the ability to build relationships with their clients, prospects, fans, friends, partners—anyone in their circle of influence and interest.

> Things are changing rapidly in the world, and brands that hope to continue to thrive are those that welcome change as an opportunity to build an advantage.

Change and Evolution

Things are changing rapidly in the world, and brands that hope to continue to thrive are those that welcome change as an opportunity to build an advantage. Torben Rick writes, "Companies most likely to be successful in making change work to their advantage are the ones that no longer view change as a discrete event to be managed, but as a constant opportunity to evolve the business." Social media presents an opportunity for you and your business to evolve.

At the time of this writing, a dramatic change has just occurred in how search engine results are weighed, basing them on one's social connections. We've all heard the term SEO (search engine optimization) used to describe how we work with Google, Bing, or Yahoo, but this has evolved. Our social relationships play into it now in exciting ways. Now, if you live in Charlotte and search online for the "best sushi in Charlotte," and you are friends on social media with Suzy, Sam, and Sally (who also love sushi), it is very possible that their favorites or top-rated sushi restaurants will pop up at the top of the list the search engine shows you. Why? Because the search engine knows that you are connected with Suzy, Sam, and Sally, and has identified their favorites online. I call this "social SEO."

What does this mean to you as a brand? Well, if you are The Rescue Mission in Tacoma, (https://www.rescue-mission.org, a client of MCP), Washington, trying to alert people to the fact that you are helping people in dire need there, the more people you are connected with through social media, the greater the odds of your mission showing up high in search results and general searches. Social media can dramatically improve your position in searches. This presents an incredible opportunity for the brand with a powerful social media presence.

Here are just a few organizations we have been able to help establish such a presence:

Teen Choice Tour

We worked with an organization called Teen Choice on their annual *Teen Choice Awards Tour*, associated with the awards show on Fox. The *Teen Choice Awards* are just that; teenagers vote for their favorite movies, TV shows, songs, actors, bands, professional athletes and so on, and awards are presented to the winners. The demographic is teens, tweens, and those in their twenties. Our job was to work with them to engage their audience, to let them know they can see their favorite Olympic gymnasts, bands, and other celebrities in a city near them.

How do we get the word out? In part, thanks to a young lady on our team who speaks the "LOL and OMG" language of this demographic, we are engaging the teen, tween, and twenties audience and their influencers, spreading the word effectively. Awareness was great and numbers were through the roof, so we were very successful. Why? Because we didn't forget that while we were communicating, building relationships (connecting), and getting the target audience very excited about seeing their favorite celebrities in their area, we still needed to move tickets to the forty-five venues and dates of the tour. We geared everything we did to selling tickets (conversion).

Our most recent statistics show that 64 percent of the people who hit the website to purchase tickets came from social media sources. So we can directly correlate the relationships we are building with the teens, tweens, and twenties audience with ticket sales. This underlines the importance of never losing sight of what your big goal is.

Companies and organizations can get very excited about tweets, retweets, posts, comments, likes and numbers of followers, but they must never lose sight of what their big goal is. When the CEO of the Teen Choice Tour calls me, he may well think all the relationship and engagement data are great, but the key question he will quickly ask is, "Are we moving tickets?" At the end of the day, you have to stay focused on your big goal. We were glad to show this CEO that we were knocking it out of the park, both in building engagement and relationship with the audience, and in ticket sales.

Joel Osteen Interactive Webcast

In 2011, we helped produce a live, interactive webcast with Joel Osteen Ministries. We were able to measure the number of viewers by the web traffic to this webcast, and it was historic. In fact, it was the largest ever live, interactive faith-based event in the history of the Internet. Not only was the message delivered, and people acknowledged they were inspired and wanted to make a change in their lives, but we connected with more people than ever before through the Internet. Through social media, we made an incredible difference in many people's lives. In 2012, we once again produced the webcast for Osteen's Washington, DC, event, and the numbers surpassed those from 2011 by another 50 percent. In 2013 our Miami Osteen event surpassed DC's by 150 percent.

Food for the Hungry

At a recent breakfast with the Director of Digital Media Marketing of the nonprofit, Food for the Hungry, we discussed their numbers, which were up—their traffic was up and their engagement was up. He expressed how happy they were with the way we are engaging and using social media as a combined team, and was grateful for our detailed reporting, transparency, and honesty. He reported to me that they were just ecstatic and committed to continuing the relationship for a long time. With stats like these after several months of working with us, it is no wonder they were so pleased:

- Social media drove 36 percent more unique visitors to their website. (Over the course of six months, they averaged a 25 percent increase in visitors to their website.)
- Social media follows and likes went up 25 percent.
- Twenty-three percent of their content on Twitter is being retweeted, so nearly one of every four tweets is being shared with a secondary audience.

In a particularly creative use of the power of social media, they took some high profile, influential bloggers to Ethiopia with them to show them the dire needs they are meeting in that area of the world. The bloggers sent back live reports and blog articles about their trip, and their personal "real sets of eyes" accounts were powerful and compelling.

In addition, the bloggers hosted an hour-long live Twitter event, tweeting from Ethiopia, allowing people to interact with them and ask questions in real time. The live event was so popular that two terms they used trended globally that day: #fhbloggers and #ethiopia. This is unheard of (and we still have the screenshot to prove it!). This brought unprecedented awareness to the work of Food for the Hungry and Ethiopia that day—all through the Twitter platform.

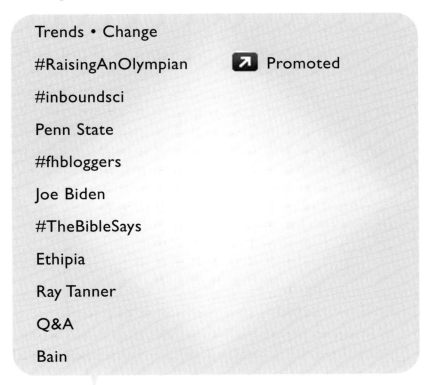

Trends • Change

#RaisingAnOlympian   ↗ Promoted

#inboundsci

Penn State

#fhbloggers

Joe Biden

#TheBibleSays

Ethipia

Ray Tanner

Q&A

Bain

The social media success of the organizations named previously was not random luck, but based in what I like to call the three C's (which you will read about in Chapter 2).

> Many wrongly assume that social media is all about gaining tens or hundreds of thousands, even millions of followers on Twitter or likes on Facebook, making them easy prey for fast-talking, self-styled social media gurus who dazzle them with schemes to deliver the big numbers.

Misconceptions about Social Media
It Is a Numbers Game

It is important to address the misconceptions about social media, especially the numbers issue. Many wrongly assume that social media is all about gaining tens or hundreds of thousands, even millions of followers on Twitter or likes on Facebook, making them easy prey for fast-talking, self-styled social media gurus who dazzle them with schemes to deliver the big numbers. Though numbers are important for weighing success in social media, they mean far less when they have been grown artificially, by way of techniques and methods that are less than ethical (for example, paying people to like their page or follow). Such ill-gotten big numbers tend to lead to a miniscule conversion rate.

My friend and author Phil Cooke (http://philcooke.com) recently wrote a blog post about some of the methods that less than ethical "consultants" use to get likes, "If you love Jesus, like this post" (http://philcooke.com/if-you-love-jesus-like-this-post/). In his blog, he writes: "'Liking' pages is one thing, 'liking' stupid, cute, or trite sayings is something else entirely. Plus, there's no real two-way conversation happening." It's a shame that some executives are blinded by the promise of big numbers. You don't need to have the following of Lady Gaga for social media to have a successful impact on your brand.

Far more important than sheer numbers is for your organization or company to target those who have an alignment with who you are. It is far better to have 10,000 Facebook friends who are in the same category or aligned with your values or a common interest than 100,000 random robot followers from around the world. As a company committed to integrity, transparency, and bringing our clients measurable results over time, it is hard to watch "consultants" and organizations that promise big numbers fast, but use a mixed bag of tricks and schemes and deliver literally no conversion. Sadly, even in the faith-based space, there are organizations that do not operate transparently, with integrity. (We hear this all too often.)

> Anyone who truly knows what they are doing in social media knows that merely going after numbers is a foolish approach when using a medium like social media that is all about communication and connection—all about relationship.

Anyone who truly knows what they are doing in social media knows that merely going after numbers is a foolish approach when using a medium like social media that is all about communication and connection—all about relationship. I promise you that big numbers of friends, followers, and likes alone won't make you more money. When the smart CEO is approached by the fast-talking consultant, promising big numbers and claiming, "I can get you 300,000 likes," he or she must ask: "Okay, but what will the conversion rate be? How will this meet my ROI objectives? How will we make money?" The conversion rate and financial goals should all be clear right from the start.

Not long ago, we were in Nashville, meeting with a new client, an author who wanted to sell more of her already successful books. We took her through the same exercise we take all our clients through:

1) What are your goals?
2) Here is how we will work to help you meet those goals through social media.
3) Here is how we will measure success (which will always tie back to the goals).

This particular author not only wanted to build a bigger audience, but she wanted to sell her books. We left the meeting and wrote up the plan, making it all clear right up front. This is crazy, crazy important. An organization that operates in integrity will take you through a similar process.

An Intern Can Handle It

I recall following the social media feed of a widely respected, large global ministry. It is a well-known brand that hundreds of thousands of people think highly of, and its legacy stretches back over dozens of years. Unfortunately, I noticed that they had a less than impressive social media presence. They were failing to engage, the text of the posts they were sending out was not well thought-out, and there just seemed to be no rhyme or reason to what they were doing or how they were using social media. I found my way to a decision maker in the organization and asked who was handling their social media. It turned out they were using a young intern to handle all their social media—a part-time intern.

So this very highly respected global brand had handed over their social media presence to a part-time intern. I let them know that this was a problem—one that needed to be corrected, and fast. If they did not act quickly, their brand would suffer.

Companies spend crazy amounts of money to ensure their corporate image is impeccable, sparing no expense on their logos, advertising, taglines, and the rest. After investing a fortune to build their image, brand, and reputation, and after being in business or ministry for decades, why in the world would such organizations risk it all by handing it over to an intern to manage? They failed to understand that people communicate through social media now, and that it is the number one way people will interact with their brand. If they understood this, there is no way they would have entrusted it to a rookie. Yet as I travel across this country and around the world, more often than not, this is exactly what I see happening.

> Social media takes time and careful,
> strategic thought. It doesn't happen by accident.
>
> If done correctly, with a sufficient investment
> of time and strategic thought, social media
> can be very good for your brand and
> even revolutionize your business.

Dabbling Is Enough

Social media takes time and careful, strategic thought. It doesn't happen by accident. It certainly doesn't happen with an investment of five to ten minutes a day, or sending out a random tweet every so often. If it is done incorrectly, it can cause damage to your brand. Unfortunately, you need to pay attention and get in with a substantial commitment of time and resources, or get out. (The only thing worse than a poor social media presence is an abandoned presence, left to fester.)

If done correctly, with a sufficient investment of time and strategic thought, social media can be very good for your brand and even revolutionize your business. It can change the outcome for your company and make you very successful. In this book, you'll learn tactics that work, with real-life accounts of how organizations that have embraced social media expanded their brands and achieved key business objectives.

CHAPTER 2

Three C's of Social Media Success

"The absolute fundamental aim is
to make money out of satisfying customers."
—John Egan

Communication, connection, and conversion. Social media success is found in communicating your message, connecting with your audience, and converting them to customers, donors, or partners. Every business and organization wants to communicate its message effectively, connect with their audience directly, and convert them to customers. That is the upside. When you satisfy your friends and followers with quality communication and genuine connection, they will reward you by converting.

Social media success is found in communicating
your message, connecting with your audience, and
converting them to customers, donors, or partners

Every character you put out has to measure to one of
the three C's: communication, connection, or conversion.

The downside is, if you do not do all three C's well, you will fail. You cannot tweet for the heck of it and hope for the best. You cannot just throw social media at the wall and hope something sticks. Every character you put out has to measure to one of the three C's: communication, connection, or conversion.

Communication

Over 50 percent of Americans own smartphones, and the number is growing by leaps and bounds. I've been fortunate to travel to India every summer for the past few years, teaching social media strategies and tactics to leaders in Chennai, Hyderabad, Mumbai, and Delhi, to name a few. The first year I was there, clamshell phones were popular and the social media platform Orkut (http://orkut.com) was the leading platform of choice. The next year, smartphones were more prevalent, and Facebook had over-taken Orkut in popularity. This goes to show, the ability to get at information and search is at our fingertips like never before.

My wife is a runner, and not long ago, we were standing in the staging area for runners of Disney's popular marathon, Goofy's Race and a Half Challenge. The DJ played a song over the sound system that I immediately loved, so I wanted to know the name of it and the artist performing it. I pulled out my smartphone and activated the Shazam app. Within seconds, the app identified the song, the Indian artist who performed it, and then gave me the option to immediately purchase the song. Several days later, Shazam sent me an e-mail reminding me that I tagged the song—and gave me an easy-to-click link so I could buy it on the spot. The fact that I can do this is simply amazing (I'm not jaded at all!), and more and more people in the U.S. are gaining the ability to get the information they want on demand from the great social media cloud that now exists.

> As a brand, if you are not present in this rapidly growing social cloud, you are simply going to become invisible, unable to be found.

@brianboyd

> Old media—direct mail, TV or radio spots,
> and the like—is not enough...not anymore.

As a brand, if you are not present in this rapidly growing social cloud, you are simply going to become invisible, unable to be found. This is where people are going for information now, which is precisely why you need to add social media or new media marketing to your existing marketing strategy mix. Old media—direct mail, TV or radio spots, and the like—is not enough...not anymore.

The Teen Choice Tour marketing team learned this after real-locating significant resources from traditional marketing mediums to social media and experiencing tremendous results in traffic and conversions. Brands that communicate in social media will be the ones that successfully extend, grow, and get more customers. They will simply reach more people, and the demographic is ever growing and broadening.

Not long ago, the woman who cuts my hair told me about her thirteen-year-old daughter who was using social media so much she wasn't getting her homework done (a common challenge for parents today). They had to cut her back on it a bit. But social media is not just for kids. (That ended about the time when MySpace gave way to Facebook.) My mother is seventy-seven years old, and she meets with friends in a prayer group on Skype once a week. She keeps in touch with our family through Facebook. This is how we communicate, more often than by phone. The age range from thirteen to seventy-seven is pretty wide. The brands that are communicating in social media are connecting with this broad demographic.

> Communicating information about your brand, your audience, your customers, your successes, and more that actually add value to the conversation that is happening.

Connection

When I refer to communicating and connecting, I don't mean simply talking about the temperature outside and sharing innocuous information on social media platforms (though that may work for the Weather Channel). I mean communicating information about your brand, your audience, your customers, your successes, and more that actually add value to the conversation that is happening.

> The more good original content you generate that connects with readers so well that they click through to your website, the greater the chance you will realize the final C, conversion to a customer or donor.

Everything you put out on social media is not seen by everybody. In fact, the life of a tweet is only a couple minutes. Your post on your Facebook page reaches only a small percentage of your fans. So though the odds of you connecting with the "right" person may not be phenomenal for every tweet or post, the more good original content you generate that connects with readers so well that they click through to your website, the greater the chance you will realize the final C, conversion to a customer or donor.

There are thousands of ways for your brand to communicate in a way that engages the audience, creating a connection. Not long ago, the work of the *Good Morning America* social media team caught my eye. Every morning, they were posting this on their Facebook page: "Good morning, America! Who do you want to say good morning to?" Many people commented, as this is a post designed simply to get people to engage, to connect. This was a solid idea.

One of our clients, a global publisher based in New York and Nashville, posted this not long ago: "If you were to write a book, what would it be about?" More people interacted with this post than any other that entire year. It really got people thinking and responding. The publisher was then able to interact with them. I liked this post because I know that those with a dream of becoming a published author rarely get the opportunity to engage directly with a major publisher, to share what they would write about. A publisher was actually listening to these authors and their ideas. It was a novel, meaningful post, and it held tremendous value for their audience.

> The idea of connection is that as people respond to your post or tweet, you reply and engage with them.

The idea of connection is that as people respond to your post or tweet, you reply and engage with them. If Jim responds to one of your posts, saying: "I totally disagree with that last statement. You guys are totally making stuff up," you don't just leave it there. You enter the conversation, saying something like, "Jim, what about that post did you not like?" Or say Jim leaves this post on one of your restaurant's social platforms: "I had a horrible experience last night at your restaurant. The food was cold and the wait staff was rude." You could enter the conversation and respond with something like this: "Jim, I am so sorry to hear of your negative experience. Obviously this is not what we want for our customers. Give me a call directly and we'll sort this out." Communication like this holds tremendous value for your brand.

A recent experience my family and I had at the Hilton Orlando *Bonnet Creek* resort (@BonnetCreek) illustrates connection perfectly. We were staying at the resort near Disney World because my wife, Fran (@FranPaceBoyd), was running both the half and full marathon in two days, Goofy's Race and a Half Challenge. When we walked into the resort lobby, we were blown away by the excitement their staff showed towards us and everyone else who was participating in the Disney marathons. They held all kinds of festivities, free food, and fun.

We had to get up the next morning at 2 a.m. to get Fran to the 3 a.m. bus that would take her to the marathon staging area. When we walked into the lobby at 2:55 a.m., the Hilton had a full (healthy) buffet set out, and balloons, signs, and banners were everywhere. Their staff members were all gathered, wearing marathon shirts, rooting on all the runners with clapping, cheers, and shouts: "Go! Go! Go!" It was extremely moving; there was so much love in it all. I remember saying to my wife: "Look at all these employees and how dedicated they are. They got up at 3 a.m. to root on their guests. More brands should be like this." It was just so impressive. When I recall it now, I still get choked up.

They also had a contest running. If you saw one of their staff members in the marathon and approached him or her to pose for a picture, you would be given a little ticket you could redeem for a prize. In the marathon, Fran ran into one of their staff members, Shadi, and had her picture taken with him, so he gave her one of the tickets. The Hilton posted Fran's picture with Shadi up on their Facebook page, and my wife tagged herself in it. A huge number of people left comments, saying they thought it was awesome, how great Hilton hotels are, and how wonderfully the resort had taken care of and cheered on the runners.

> Don't miss this:
> Due to our mutual engagement on social media,
> we gained a potential client.

Later that day as I stood in the lobby, a young lady walked up to me and asked, "Are you Brian Boyd?" I let her know I was. She said: "Well, I'm with the Hilton and we saw that you posted to our page. Thank you for liking our page, and thank you for staying at the Hilton. You are a valued guest and we are so happy you're here." Then she asked, "Is there anything we can do to make your stay more enjoyable?" I complimented her and the hotel staff and it led to a conversation. She asked me about my profession, one thing led to another and we scheduled a call to consult with them on social media. Don't miss this: Due to our mutual engagement on social media, we gained a potential client.

I was blown away by the way the online crosses to the offline. The Hilton saw the positive comment I posted to their Facebook page (their online social media presence), and then they saw me in the lobby and connected with me, telling me I was a valued customer. The whole 360 of this was pretty amazing. You better believe that we have not only told everyone we know of how awesome this Hilton was, but we will also likely never stay in a Disney hotel again—we're staying at the Hilton Orlando Bonnet Creek.

> Conversion is the name of the game.
> You can communicate and you can connect,
> but eventually you have to get the conversion.

Conversion

Conversion is the name of the game. You can communicate and you can connect, but eventually you have to get the conversion. It's hard for me to think of any brand, whether a personal executive or company brand, where it is not important to gain conversions. At the end of the day, you must get conversions. What do I mean by conversion? It could be people signing up for your e-mail list, going into your sales lead funnel (ROR funnel), subscribing to a service you offer, or going to a web page and clicking on an item to buy.

We handle social media for Jules Radino, the drummer for Blue Oyster Cult. He has a business plan that I believe is going to make him a rock star (pun intended), and built a website where he offers one-on-one drum lessons over the Internet. Though our social media strategy includes communicating and connecting with his audience, the goal is to get people to convert—to go to his site to subscribe to online drum lessons with a great drummer.

In one area of our work with Joel Osteen Ministries (@JoelOsteen), a conversion occurred when people participating in a live webcast event went to a web page and left their e-mail address, name, and other information, indicating, "I made a decision tonight while interacting with your event and I would like to share this with you." The ministry would then send them more information about their decision and what they learned through the webcast, while gaining testimonial content for social media.

For a nonprofit client like Food for the Hungry (@food4thehungry), conversion could be gaining donations for a campaign or operation in a certain part of the country or world where they are reaching out and helping others. Conversion can vary widely, depending on the organization and its goals. For the Teen Choice Tour, selling tickets to an event is conversion. For a ministry, gaining response to their message could be conversion. For OneHope (@FollowOneHope), a client of ours who educates and helps people around the world, conversion could be gaining gifts in kind, engaging volunteers to help in the work of their ministry.

In fact, OneHope offers a textbook example of how the entire cycle of social media works—communication, connection, and conversion. Before OneHope became a customer of ours, they were a connection. We had followed them on social media, attended some of their conferences, and built a relationship with them, both online and offline. So when someone we worked with on their staff called us at the end of the year, asking us to give a generous gift and partner with them in their work in a certain country, we were glad to give.

> At Media Connect Partners (MCP), we never lose sight of the fact that we work for people at the executive level of the brands we serve.

At Media Connect Partners (MCP), we never lose sight of the fact that we work for people at the executive level of the brands we serve. And people at that level need to know what they are getting from their social media investment. When we give our clients their monthly reports, conversion data goes right on top, showing how their goals were met. So even if executives read nothing else, at least they will see what is most important to them. Though they can then drill down into the follows, likes, tweets, retweets, and more, at the end of the day, it is all about conversion and helping our clients achieve their goals.

Minutes before writing this, I was in a phone conversation with the COO of one of our major clients. He is the final decision maker—the man who "cuts the checks." We do not speak every day, but I make sure that we talk every month or so to ensure MCP is meeting his goals. Although he stays at an altitude of 10,000 feet in regard to the "social media project," he made one huge point with me: "Brian, what I really love about you and your team is your reporting. You show me our conversions and growth using graphs I can immediately grasp and share." It's all about conversions. This is what the COO needs to see.

CHAPTER 3

Know Your Goals

> "If you want to be successful in business, you've got to ask yourself two questions. Ask them over and over again. 'What business are we in?' and 'How's business?'"
>
> —Peter Drucker

> "We have to move to new media (i.e., social media), because with traditional media, I can't tell who sees our ads. I can't measure success."
>
> —Rolf Zettersten, senior vice president and publisher, Hachette Book Group

Many times, our first meetings with potential clients go something like this:

"Hey, we've stepped into social media and spent a lot of money to fund and resource it (or "found an intern to run it"), but we aren't getting any results. What's that about?"

"Well, what are you trying to achieve? What are your goals?"

"Uhh...." They cannot immediately state their goals.

"Well, can you give us a look at your written plan?"

"Umm...."

They have no written goals for social media. In fact, usually it begins with about as much thought and consideration as this:

"Facebook is the place to be! Everybody's there, and it's fun!" (2008)

"Twitter is where it's at! Let's get tweeting!" (2009)

"Everybody is into Pinterest! Let's get pinning!" (2010)

"Instagram is hot! Let's start posting pics!" (2011)

> "Social media is cool and everyone is doing it, so we need to do it as well," is simply not good enough.

"Social media is cool and everyone is doing it, so we need to do it as well," is simply not good enough. Many organizations put anything out on social media with no goal in mind—a kind of "throw it at the wall and see what sticks" approach. Goals are key to the growth of any business. And, just as in any form of marketing and PR, it is essential to have measurable goals for social media. You must have a clear view of what success looks like, what you hope to get out of social media, and how you will measure success.

> No matter what posts you put out and no matter which platforms you choose, make sure they have something to do with a goal of your company or organization.

It is essential that you have a written plan with clear goals and a comprehensive strategy for reaching them. It is also essential

@brianboyd

that the majority of your social media communication ties back to your organization's goals. An occasional one-off message like, "Wow, it's an icy day outside!" is fine. But if you are putting out ten pieces of original content per day, across three to four different platforms, a big percentage of that content should relate back to your goals. Even if you read and do nothing else in this book, you will be well on the way to success if you follow this one rule: No matter what posts you put out and no matter which platforms you choose, make sure they have something to do with a goal of your company or organization.

Just as you would not think about building a house without a set of blueprints, or creating a company without a business plan, your social media plan must begin with a strong set of clear goals. After all, you can only measure success by how well you have achieved your goals. And though it is tempting to think so, the number of likes, followers, and friends themselves are not always indicators of success.

For Teen Choice, as you read in the previous chapter, the primary goals were connection with their audience and ticket sales for their live tour events. The goals of Food for the Hungry were to receive donations and gifts in kind commitments. *Prevention* magazine sought content ideas from readers that they might not have thought of. So what are your goals?

You'll need to sit down with your executive team, whiteboard out some goals, and generate a written social media strategy. Helping our clients to develop their comprehensive social strategy is our favorite part of working with them. First, we help them to define their goals. Then we help them build their social media strategy. Finally, we help them choose the social platforms that fit best with their strategy and map them to their goals.

Here is an overview of that process:

Step 1—Take a good hard look at what your "competitors" are doing in the social media space.

Media Connect Partners (MCP) created the "MCP Social Competitive Matrix" tool to evaluate a brand against its competition. This analysis can be done at the beginning of the process, then again at milestones throughout your strategy's execution to measure how well you are doing.

Social Media Effectiveness Criteria	Company 1	Company 2	Company 3	Company 4	Company 5
Strategy	3.8	0	3	3.5	4
Execution	3.8	0	3.5	3.8	4
Interaction with Fans	3.2	0	3.6	4.2	4.1
Use of 70/30 Rule	3	0	3.5	3.5	4.3
Brand Consistency	4.2	0	4	4.5	4.8
Twitter Presence Strength	3	0	3.5	3.8	3.8
Facebook Presence Strength	3.2	0.5	3.8	4	4.2
Pinterest Presence Strength	3.5	0	3.8	3.5	3.6
Instagram Presence Strength	0	0	0	1	3.6
YouTube Presence Strength	3.9	0	2	4.5	3.2
LinkedIn Presence Strength	1	1	2	1	1
Response Timeliness	2.5	0	2.8	3.8	4.2
Post Frequency	3	0	2.5	4	3.9
Average Rank	2.9	0.1	2.9	3.5	3.7

Key

0 = None/ Red	1 = Poor/ Red	2 = Fair/ Yellow	3 = Good/ Yellow	4 = Very Good/ Green	5 = Excellent/ Green

- What are they doing well? What are they doing poorly?
- What are they doing that is effective? What are they doing that is ineffective?
- Armed with some analysis of what others in your space are doing, take this back to your goals.

Step 2—Think about your goals—organizational goals, not merely marketing goals. What are you trying to do?

At this stage, think about your company's goals. Don't get hung up thinking about only your social media goals. In chapters 4 and 8, we will define how to create social media strategies which map to your goals.

@brianboyd

Step 3—Create large buckets and put goals in them.

You may have a long list of goals. Though you cannot build a strategy for each one, it is good to move as many goals as possible into buckets.

Draw three big circles on a whiteboard. List all your goals and put them into groups (buckets) within these circles.

If your goal is awareness (getting the message out on who you are), you would write down things like this: word of mouth, website visits, e-mail opt-ins, newsletter signups, and so on. If your goal is sales, write that down.

Recently, we met with an organization in the arts space and brainstormed their goals with them. One of their senior team members raised her hand and said: "I have a goal. We want to feel loved." When I asked what she meant by this, she replied: "All our competitors get mentioned in news coverage—this charity, that charity, and the other—but we're right here, local to them, and they never mention us." Sometimes it is a goal to get some love from the mainstream media.

Set Your Targets

Once you establish your goals, it is time to set your targets. Goals are what is important to you as an organization: making a certain amount of sales, gaining a certain number of relationships, getting a certain number of people signed to your mailing list, reaching a set amount of gross sales per year, and so on. Targets may be how you get there. For example, the number of people you need to add to your sales pipeline, the number of ad impressions you need, the number of people who need to see your brand, and so on.

We serve a big church in the Tacoma, Washington, area and we set targets for them because they need to know what to expect in 2013. We set targets for likes, retweets, interactions, comments, and more, and we hold ourselves to them to try to beat these numbers. These targets all relate back to goals we established.

Measure Social Media Effectiveness in Order to Manage It

You must be able to measure how well you are meeting your goals and the effectiveness of your strategies. Our company's motto is "Measure Everything," and it should be yours as well.

ROI (return on investment)

There are tools available that allow you to build analytics to measure how well you are doing with social media. For our clients, we make sure that anytime they put a link in any post, when someone clicks on it, we can immediately tell: who clicked it, where the click came from, where they were clicking to, how many clickthroughs, and much more. In this way we get fast ROI results to clients. We know which posts did well, which ones did not, which ones led to more donations, and much more.

We have twenty to twenty-five different metrics we measure for our clients, which we include in a report to show their ROI for each social media platform. We can show friends, followers, likes, retweets, celebrity retweets, conversations, clickthroughs, e-mail opt-ins, sentiment, purchases, donations, and more. Each organization has its own set of unique ROI metrics and measures, and we help them come up with theirs.

> Every instinct we have in a face-to-face opportunity to build a relationship with a customer can be achieved through social media.

ROR (return on relationship)

Every instinct we have in a face-to-face opportunity to build a relationship with a customer can be achieved through social media…and we can measure it. How do we know if what we are doing in personal encounters is working? Easy. Relationships are not theoretical.

> Social media is best understood as a relationship catalyst.

> We place the cart before the horse when we expect social media to function as a cash register.

Handshakes on the sales floor precede deals. Trust comes before a purchase. Engagement precedes exchange. We believe social media is best understood as a relationship catalyst. We can move customers closer to the point of sale. We place the cart before the horse when we expect social media to function as a cash register. Whether your goal is to get donations or enlist volunteer help, you can't get there without relationship.

Some time ago, a good friend of mine called me. He works for a large global nonprofit. He said, "Brian, it's the end of the year and we've got a campaign that's winding down, and we're trying to hit a certain number." He then explained to me what they were doing, how well it was working, and asked if I would consider contributing to their campaign. I said I would love to. My wife and I decided on an amount, we cut a check, and mailed it to the organization.

Had I simply received a postcard, or even a slick mailer in the mail that said, "Give to our campaign," I probably would have just looked at it a second and thrown it away. The difference was I had a relationship with this man, so I gave.

To build your ROR, you must ask yourself these key questions:

- Does this execution bring us closer to the customer?
- Do customers know more about our products because of this copy?
- Have we improved relationships as a direct result of our last six months of social media efforts?

You build relationship through social media over time by interacting, posting, being real and transparent, talking about others more than yourself, telling your business (or nonprofit's) story, asking questions, sharing concerns, and more. You build the relationship by telling stories about your organization, its work, its accomplishments, and by interacting with people's posts, tweets, or comments.

Then when you do come to "the ask" for the business, donation, or campaign, people will say: "You know, this organization means a lot to me. I'd love to help." This is ROR, return on relationship, which is exactly what social media is all about: building relationships over time, and conversion.

CHAPTER 4

Find Your Brand's Social Media Fit

> "You can't do today's job with yesterday's methods and be in business tomorrow."
>
> —George W. Bush

> "Strategy is about setting yourself apart from the competition. It's not a matter of being better at what you do— it's a matter of being different at what you do."
>
> —Michael Porter

When you build a website, you don't just start "coding." You typically start with a plan, a strategy. You lay out your content areas, build storyboards, think about the actions you want visitors to take, and create design comps. You must have a strategy and plan. The same is true for social media. By setting your social media goals, you established the foundation for your strategy. Now it is time to create a strategy and plan that will map to your goals. You need to identify and implement the social media strategies and tactics that will map to those goals.

> It is a common mistake to focus on Facebook— even if it is the 800-pound gorilla of social platforms.

Social Media—More Than Facebook

Many people think of social media and think: *Facebook*. Though I am sure Facebook loves this, just as the Coca-Cola people love that many people in the South refer to soft drinks collectively as "cokes," it is a common mistake to focus on Facebook—even if it is the 800-pound gorilla of social platforms.

An executive from a large coffee company from the Northeast contacted us and said: "Well, we've had a consultant come in. They charge less than you do and they have us on Facebook and are getting us ads on Facebook." It was all Facebook. The "consultant" was not charging that much less than we would have (and we would have established a multi-platform social media presence), and we could see from a mile away that it was the wrong strategy for this company. The organization had amazing content (videos, photos, stories, etc.) it could utilize across many better social media platforms than Facebook, with better results. They could have entrusted their social media to a legitimate consultant who engaged with them in setting social media goals, creating strategies, and forming a comprehensive plan, but opted instead for a one-trick pony outfit that cashes in on the rampant Facebook-only fixation.

Many companies and organizations have worked themselves into a frenzy building their pages, groups, likes, and comments on Facebook to the exclusion of all other platforms. It is easy to be caught up in the excitement as the likes and comments keep tallying up, but these are simply not what will pay the bills.

"You're not in business to make Facebook money, you're in business to make you money."

@brianboyd

I have had to caution many companies: "You're not in business to make Facebook money, you're in business to make you money." That is what we help our clients do. Facebook would love to have them pay a lot of money for advertising and promote posts to get more eyeballs. But they need to do this very strategically, to promote the correct kinds of posts and spend the right kinds of ad dollars. Whether posts or ads, they should drive people to campaigns which can turn them into conversions. If companies handle this incorrectly (and many do), Facebook makes money, but they do not.

Facebook is not the be-all and end-all of social media platforms. I would go even further and say you should view social media as far more than the top three in the view of many companies (at this writing): Facebook, Twitter, and LinkedIn. And though you will see in these pages that we do advise our clients to make effective use of more than one social media platform, and not to put all their social media eggs in one basket, we also emphasize the need to carefully think through which platforms to use.

Webcast for Retirees (A Cautionary Tale)

Early on in the social media days, one company we served was convinced that they needed to engage their demographic (seniors) using a webcast. They loved participating in webcasts, believed in their effectiveness, and knew that we were one of the best in the business at putting them together, so they invited us to make it happen. Though we were not convinced the platform was the best fit for their demographic and gave them better ideas for engaging it (which they did not act on), we set to work putting together an excellent webcast.

Bottom line: The webcast was well done, but the project was a failure. At the time, though seniors were engaging with some social media platforms, the webcast was not one of them. They simply did not show up for it online. (This also taught us to turn down jobs when we know that an ineffective plan is in place.) This company simply used the wrong platform to engage their demographic.

Foursquare and Free Stuff (A Success Story)

On a trip to Cozumel, my family and I wandered into what turned out to be a crazy expensive restaurant. (We sat down at the table before looking over the menu and prices.) Even the soft drinks were over $4 each—and no free refills. We figured we would just eat small, enjoy ourselves, and move on. Then my daughter got the idea of checking in on Foursquare to see if she could find a discount or a deal of some kind.

After she checked in, a special popped up for a free collector's glass. (At least there was something to take the edge off that $4 soft drink!) She flagged down the waiter who did not speak English, and finally resorted to pointing to the Foursquare screen on her phone, showing him the free collector's glass offer. The waiter called the manager over. He spoke to us briefly, then disappeared for about five minutes before returning with a giant bag of souvenirs—something we had not expected at all. Then, to top it all off, he gave us a free round of soft drinks.

Needless to say, we walked out of there feeling pretty good. After all, we had saved some money and had a huge bag of souvenirs. All this because my daughter thought to check in on Foursquare. This is an example of a business using the right platform. And it worked exactly as it is supposed to, because the next time we are over there, you can be sure we will stop in to dine and get another big bag of souvenirs.

> You should not simply jump on any and all social platforms, driven by size, popularity, how cool they are, or how much you personally love them.

You should not simply jump on any and all social platforms, driven by size, popularity, how cool they are, or how much you personally love them. Not all platforms will be a good fit for you. Here are a few things you can do to help your brand find its social media fit.

Decide which platforms you want to use.

There are thousands of social media platforms out there, far more than just Facebook, Twitter, YouTube, Instagram, and Pinterest.

Your decisions of which platforms to use for your brand are very important. Pinterest may be a good platform for some (Hobby Lobby, for instance), but Instagram may be better for others. You may not need Instagram or Pinterest if you simply need to immediately develop a blog for your company or organization. Your social media goals and strategies should inform your choice of platforms, as should the content you intend to use.

With our Teen Choice client, we knew right out of the gate that Instagram and YouTube were going to be huge platforms for them because the demographic they appeal to, ages eight to eighteen, use them like crazy. They cannot seem to get enough pictures or video! Demographics can be an incredibly valuable guide for choosing platforms.

> No matter which platforms you choose,
> be sure you are able to measure success with
> it to determine how well it works for you.

Twitter and Facebook are perfect for Joel Osteen because he makes so many pithy tweetable comments, thoughts of ten to fifteen words that take off like wildfire. Pinterest and Instagram are perfect matches for Hobby Lobby, because pictures and graphics are such a key component to their crafts and home decor content. No matter which platforms you choose, be sure you are able to measure success with it to determine how well it works for you.

Decide how you will interact with and use the platforms you choose.

After choosing the platforms you want to use, be sure you have a plan for generating content to put into them. For example, if you choose YouTube, obviously you need to generate video content. If you choose Instagram, you'll need photographic content. If you choose a blog, you'll need to regularly produce posts, stories, and articles. For each platform in your strategy, you must have a plan for creating appropriate content for them.

Remember, it is far better to focus on achieving excellence in one platform than doing a poor job on multiple platforms.

Use the platforms frequently and consistently.

One of the worst things you can do is abandon a social media platform, leaving merely a ghost presence of it on the web. You must not abandon the social media platforms you've chosen. You must have an intentional plan for regularly and consistently updating and posting to all your platforms.

A recent experience with a candidate for one of our open positions underlines the importance of this. We require all applicants to provide us with their LinkedIn account name and Twitter handle. (After all, we are a social media agency.) Typically, these are great, nicely done. But this candidate had not posted a tweet in over a year. His LinkedIn account was out of date. It would have been far better for him not to even have a Twitter or LinkedIn account than to have them out there, abandoned, and so poorly done.

@brianboyd

In social media, you must either go in all the way or get out. If you cannot provide sufficient focus on a social media platform, you need to step out of it. This is especially important since Google, Yahoo, and Bing index social media constantly, making whatever you have out there on social media either helpful or detrimental to your brand.

Create and push out high quality content consistently.

Content you create and push out on social media platforms must be of the highest quality and represent your organization well. This is another area in which some organizations fail miserably in social media—by not providing sufficient content. They may have decided they were going to be on several platforms, but had no plan (or a poor one) for who was going to write, edit, screen, and post content.

Pristine content is key to establishing an impeccable social media presence that assures potential customers or donors that what your organization does, it does with excellence. For example, when people search for an organization that helps those in need and comes upon your nonprofit, you want them to find your social media presence infused with expressions of care and compassion. Research has shown that the number one thing donors want is regular updates and evidence that their donated funds are making a difference and being put to good use—something that can be easily done through social media. In light of all this, it is impossible to overstate the importance of your brand having a well thought-out social media presence featuring consistently high quality content.

How much content should your organization anticipate creating? This varies depending on the platform. For example, if one of your platforms is a blog, you should plan on generating at least two to three high value posts, articles, or stories a week. If you are using Instagram, Twitter, or Facebook, your plan should typically include from one to four posts or updates a day, though every organization is different and this is only a baseline number.

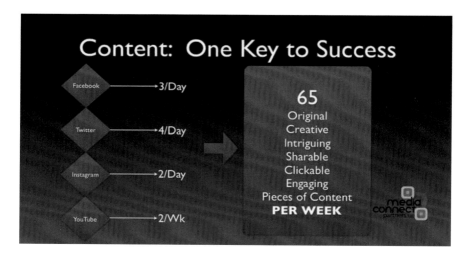

Many companies forget how much content social media requires. Social media sucks up content like a vacuum cleaner. It is important to do the math. See the graphic, "Content: One Key to Success." Notice the varying frequency for updates across the four platforms in the graphic. Also notice that this calls for *sixty-five* pieces of content per week, just over nine pieces of content in any 24-hour period. And not just any content, it must be: original, creative, intriguing, shareable, and more. This is a lot of work!

This is when the light clicks on for most brands, "Hey, this isn't going to be just a ten- minute daily thing, this is something we as a brand need to take seriously. Of course you can ramp this down or up. Some organizations do a lot more communication than this, and others less. But think how hard it is to create *sixty-five* original pieces of content that people want to share. This takes time and careful, strategic thought.

You need to have a clear plan on who will create, edit, screen, and post content. But if you jump in and cannot generate the content that is necessary and think, *Wow, I've bitten off more than I can chew*, then you need to step back and focus on just one or two platforms. It is better to be on fewer platforms with a well thought-out presence than to be on many platforms with a poor presence. You can always ramp up to other platforms as resources allow.

Content should always tie in with your goals. Though it may be fine during the holiday season to wish people well, or if there is some national tragedy, to offer thoughts and prayers, typically posts and updates should tie in with your goals.

One organization we are proud to serve helps feed people all over the world. With them, we turned everyone in their worldwide organization into a content expert. We helped them build a cloud-based website they can access to upload stories, pictures, videos, and news. So when any member of their organization sees something happening in the field, has a great story to share, or sees something they need to bring attention to, they can submit the content to the website. From there, it is added to a queue for processing and review. After it receives the official okay, it is then published across social platforms. In this way they get to tell their story, show donors their money at work, inspire volunteers with the fruits of their labors, and offer humanity, transparency, reality, and compassion. This works phenomenally well, and in near real time.

Rolling with Platform Changes and Evolution

Think of the many times Facebook has changed its look, feel, and privacy policies. In early 2013, Facebook launched its Graph Search, raising widespread privacy concerns among users. Not long before this writing, Instagram made a major change to its privacy policy, saying in essence, "We have the right to sell your photos and not give you money for them." (After a mass exodus of users from the service, Instagram revised its policy.) Such changes leave an opening for competitive newer platforms, like Medium (a new platform at the time of this writing), to address these concerns and shift the social media balance. One thing remains constant among all social media platforms—they are bound to change.

In fact, social media is changing on a daily basis. As new platforms develop, new technologies emerge, and existing platforms change their rules and monetization policies, we can certainly expect shifts. In any twelve-month period, you will see four or five dynamic shifts in how people move their content around. Just as anyone who specializes in SEO and keywords knows that a good chunk of their job must be keeping up with Google's ever-changing algorithm (as well as those of Bing and Yahoo), anyone who uses social media platforms must know that a good chunk of their job will be keeping up with social platforms as they change and evolve.

Social media marketing will test your entrepreneurial drive, exercise it, and make it stronger. "The entrepreneur always searches for change, responds to it, and exploits it as an opportunity" (Peter Drucker). Those with the entrepreneurial spirit always see change as an opportunity. Consider yourself blessed with that spirit if you recognize the incredible opportunity social media offers your brand and you are chomping at the bit to roll with social platform changes. If you possess the entrepreneurial spirit, but lack the time and resources to keep up with the changes, be sure to get expert help in doing so...or risk falling behind.

CHAPTER 5

Content Is King

"Those who succeed will propel the Internet forward as a marketplace of ideas, experiences, and products— a marketplace of content."
—Bill Gates (January 3, 1996)

"If consumers like a company's story, they are often willing to give its product or service a try."
—MP Mueller

Cliché warning: Content is king. Content is the currency of social media. Content drives your brand, and businesses with a wealth of fresh, original content will prosper in social media. Even better, as content quality increases, ROI increases. When you provide good content the numbers will come. This is the upside.

Content is the currency of social media. Content drives your brand, and businesses with a wealth of fresh, original content will prosper in social media.

When you provide good content the numbers will come.

The downside is, social media takes time to bear fruit and sucks up huge amounts of content. Your concerted social media efforts today will typically benefit your brand four to six months down the road. Though there are exceptions, it just doesn't happen overnight. Brands love when content goes viral quickly, bringing immediate results, but these are exceptions, not the rule. This is why we encourage all our clients to buckle in for the long haul, stick to it, wear the white hat, and refuse to resort to gimmicks and schemes.

Create a *lot* of good content, talk about others, talk about your company and the things you do in an engaging way—do all the things we advise you to do—and you will find that over time, social media will prove effective in growing your numbers, building engagement, and increasing the ROI points you have developed to define success. You will also find that few things do more to build your brand than effective, engaging, consistently excellent social media content.

Four Ways Social Media Will Bring Success to Your Brand

Not long ago, I enjoyed watching an NBA basketball game from a luxury suite. A man sitting beside me introduced himself, and I told him who I was. He asked me what I did and I told him I owned a social agency. His interest was piqued.

> "No way! I am the COO of an organization, and just today we were talking about how much we needed a social media plan."

> I stuck out my hand and said with a smile, "Glad to meet you!"

> "We're an accounting firm," he said. "Frankly, we don't know why social media is important for us, but we know we need to be there."

"It's really clear why you need to be there," I said. "First, an accounting firm the size of yours needs to be seen as a thought leader. When people in the industry ask, 'Who can I go to for solid advice?' and 'Who is a thought leader in this industry?' they need to think of you first. You need to be in that place. If you can put out good content nuggets consistently—on changes in tax law, the president's new tax plan, updates in state tax reform and the like—over time, people will realize that your organization really knows what it's talking about. It will become a thought leader through consistent, strategic content creation and publishing."

"Second," I continued, "the kind of content you put out makes your existing customers happy. They want to know they've chosen a great accounting firm. In between the times when they talk with one of your representatives, they can follow your corporate blog and social media platforms and continually glean valuable information that burns into their brain how great your firm is. It tells them you are looking out for them, staying up to speed, and that as changes happen in the world, you're on top of them. This reassures your existing customers that they have chosen the right partner."

By this time, he was starting to get it.

"Third, all your non-customers see what is going on, that your firm knows what it is talking about and understands what is happening in the world. They compare your firm to their firm that doesn't do these things and decide to give you a call. So it will bring in new business for you."

I definitely had his interest now.

"This doesn't happen simply because you push out a few tweets every day. It comes by strategically thinking through the types of bite-size, easily shareable content you'll create; content that will communicate, connect, and convert to meet your goals."

> The only way your brand will grow in following, engagement, and interactions is with consistent, great, original content.

The only way your brand will grow in following, engagement, and interactions is with consistent, great, original content. Though there are plenty of black hat organizations out there that will try to sell you on gimmicks (like "buying" followers), when it comes down to it, only when you're wearing the white hat and doing things the right way can we guarantee you'll have a growing, interactive, engaging following that ends up doing that final C, and converting.

> If your company or organization is consistent in putting out solid, original content through social media:
>
> - You will expand your reach.
>
> - Your content will be shared more often.
>
> - People will view you as a thought leader.
>
> - People will value your humanity and transparency.

@brianboyd

We won't break down all the science of it and get into all the algorithms that show why the Internet loves fresh new content. The fundamentals are simple. If your company or organization is consistent in putting out solid, original content through social media:

- You will expand your reach.
- Your content will be shared more often.
- People will view you as a thought leader.
- People will value your humanity and transparency. (They will like you and therefore want to do business with or support you.)

Who Are the Content Experts?

Many times, new clients will come to us and say: "Hey, we're ready to go. We'll be engaging you through strategy and community development. Now, go figure out what you're going to say for us." We are quick to say: "Whoa! We are experts in what we know, but not in what you know. That's your area of expertise. We need to rely on you for that content."

It would be wrong of us to partner with an organization and presume we know their business better than they do. It can also intimidate the social media people on staff who are already concerned: "Consultants are doing my job! What will happen to me?" Besides, early on in our business, we were less than successful in trying to create content out of thin air for clients. We know what works in social media, but we simply are not experts in cooking, feeding the hungry, accounting, publishing, and the many other areas in which our clients are experts. We turn the people we work with in the client's organization into advocates, and work together with them to succeed. They toss the raw content over the fence to us and we take it, cut it up, shape it, and distribute it across all their social media platforms. The object is to get the team to toss the social raw content over the fence to the social media team.

One client of ours, Food for the Hungry (FH), has offices and personnel around the globe, and is expert in:

- Sheltering, feeding, and clothing survivors of natural disasters.
- Long-term development work with the poor in more than twenty-five countries, transforming impoverished communities into healthy, productive places for children to grow.

When we began constructing their social strategy, it was very exciting for us. We were able to construct an online, cloud-based system that would allow anyone on their staff, no matter where they were in the world, to submit content in real time into a "funnel" which feeds directly to the social media team. This could be raw content, anything cool, sad, serious, or interesting—a video, a Word document, a PDF, a picture or an encouraging note or letter, an e-mail forward, an URL—it all goes into the funnel. The social media team takes that content, cuts it up, and pushes it out the other end of the funnel to a variety of social media platforms. The beauty of the system is, the whole process could move very quickly, which is what most companies need and want. They want to get out exciting information that looks great that people will want to click on, virtually in real time, so that after they click on it, they will go to a landing page or website and convert.

To this day, this system continues to work very, very well for FH. On any given day, thirty or more FH staff members submit content to the funnel. They have created a culture of engagement where everyone on staff understands they are content experts and that they can help further the mission of FH by contributing quality content.

Creating a Culture of Engagement

Where Food for the Hungry has succeeded in establishing a culture of engagement, many companies and organizations have failed. We built a LinkedIn page for one such company with many employees. Despite their best efforts—even requests from the top officer in the company—only three employees (out of hundreds!) followed their new LinkedIn page. One might well conclude that either the employees hate their jobs, do not care about the company, or they do not know how to follow the page (though this last one did not seem to be the case for this company).

Another client, a large educational institution, had several hundred employees, what we call "verticals" (faculty, admissions representatives, food service staff, sports department staff, and more), who could and should have been contributing social media content, but they were not. Their employees failed to see the tremendous opportunity they had to give people a 360-degree view of how great their organization was by simply pushing out photos, videos, and other pieces of content through social media platforms. This institution had failed to foster in their verticals the reality that content was all around them, if only they would look for it.

> People tend to want to work with companies and support organizations that treat their employees well. Nothing says a company treats its employees well as when those employees take time after business hours to talk up the company on social media.

Many companies and organizations struggle to generate the quality and volume of content required to prosper and build their brand through social media because their staff members are not engaged. That's too bad because people tend to want to work with companies and support organizations that treat their employees well. Nothing says a company treats its employees well as when those employees take time after business hours to talk up the company on social media.

Here are just a few ways to create (or build) a culture of engagement:

- Include social media content contribution as an expectation in every job description. (Each of our employees is expected to contribute one blog post a month—it's in their job description.)
- Top leaders should frequently encourage content contribution, reminding staff members of the benefits of sharing the company story on social media.
- Reward content contribution with special incentives. Even a $20 gift card, or an hour or two of paid time off can go a long way in rewarding a frequent content contributor.
- Removing any barriers to entry for content. Make sure everyone knows how to contribute. Make it easy to contribute. Make sure employees know they don't have to overthink or overproduce what they contribute—anything interesting, inspiring, or cool will do, no matter how raw. We specialize in creating simple systems for companies so that contributing content via any computer or smart device is easy.

Content Is All Around You

Content is everywhere. It could be a picture of a great poster, a cool photo from a sporting event, or a heartfelt video testimonial. One of our clients, Joel Osteen Ministries, has enjoyed great feedback on the Facebook page for Osteen's book, *I Declare: 31 Promises to Speak Over Your Life*, by simply encouraging people to finish the statement: "I declare _____." We often push out a picture of someone holding a sign or feature a post that completes that statement: "I declare God's dream for my life is coming to pass...," "I declare that with God, all things are possible," and so on.

Joel Osteen has also done very well on Twitter because on any given Sunday, every one of his sermons will serve up as many as ten to twelve tweetable comments. Once tweeted, they also tend to get a lot of traction in the social media space, where they are widely retweeted and shared. For example, on January 1, 2013, Joel tweeted: "Don't go into the new year holding a grudge from last year. Leave the hurts and disappointments behind" (https://twitter.com/JoelOsteen/status/286286198610214913). This tweet has been retweeted (shared) over 10,000 times! It garnered a potential overall audience of millions.

> Any company or organization that fails to capture and funnel content to social media in this day and age will lose relevance.

Social media content is all around us. We just have to open our eyes to see it. The challenge for every brand—whether huge or small, one hundred employees or ten thousand—is capturing that content and funneling it into the social media stream. Capturing and funneling content must be seen as mission critical by every vertical in a company or organization. Any company or organization that fails to capture and funnel content to social media in this day and age will lose relevance, so the stakes could not be higher.

I've already made the point that social media sucks up an amazing amount of content, but this is worth repeating. Do the math and you quickly see just how much. If you have six platforms and need two pieces of original content for each every day, that is twelve pieces of content per day—eighty-four pieces per week. So companies need to either prioritize where to focus their efforts in social media, get ready to create, cut up, and push out a lot of original, creative content, or hire somebody to help them.

Not long ago, I spoke by phone with a COO of a very large brand with dozens of social media platforms—they have a dozen Facebook pages for their books and business opportunities alone! They had taken on too much and were underwater. The content was not good and rarely posted. In short, they were floundering. The COO was very honest with me, saying: "Brian, we just do not know what we're doing. The problem we have is that when people come onto our social media platforms and complain, or give us attaboys, we can't engage with them—we're stretched too thin!"

> It is better to do a great job on one social media platform than to jump in on several platforms and do a poor job.

As I've said before, it is best to start with just one platform, make sure you generate the quality content you need consistently, and see how it goes. Once you are doing that well, start on a second platform or blog. Then start a third platform once the other two are going well. Whatever you do, don't go underwater. I cannot stress this enough: It is better to do a great job on one social media platform than to jump in on several platforms and do a poor job.

Everyone Is a Content Contribution Expert

The strongest brands in the social media space are those whose members have embraced the idea and expectation that they are content contribution experts. In Tulsa, Oklahoma, we engaged with Oral Roberts University (@OralRobertsU). Occasionally, we have someone in the food services area take a picture of the amazing dish that is the food special and we push it out to social media. These have proven to be some of the most popular pieces of content this institution puts out! Not only can existing students not get enough of these pictures, but guess who else gets engaged? The alumnae of the institution. They love to leave posts and replies: "OMG! I remember eating that way back when I was a student there!" and "Wow! Things have sure changed since I was there!" Are these food services staff members who post these dishes trained in social media? No. Yet the content is great!

Some time ago, Oral Roberts University installed a new president, Dr. Billy Wilson (@WilsonBilly). I had the opportunity to speak with him outside one of the buildings on campus. I let him know who I was, what I do, and that I was an ORU alumnae. I asked him for a fifteen to thirty second video greeting to the alumnae that I could post to the ORU alumnae Facebook page. He readily agreed, so I took out my iPhone and right there on the spot, I shot a thirty second video of Dr. Wilson greeting the alumnae: "Hey, I am looking forward to meeting with you and hearing from you all...." This was great content. It was timely, effective, and easy to do.

Any member of a company or organization should view themselves as a social media content contribution expert, and regularly feed content to the internal social media expert. This can be done simply by merely setting up a dedicated e-mail box. Staff members can then easily toss raw content possibilities over the fence to the social media expert through that e-mail address. They don't have to think about what would make the best story, how to say it in 140 characters or any of that, they just have to faithfully toss it over to the social media expert. The expert can then choose which material works well, edit it as needed, and push it out through social media.

Great Content Will Build Your Brand; Bad Content Will Torpedo It

When content is good and well crafted, it can bring amazing results in building your brand. When content is bad or done poorly, it can torpedo your brand.

Not long ago, I was invited to travel to teach social media tactics and strategies to leaders in several cities in India. At the same time, back in the States, we were running social media for a huge product launch by one of our clients, a pharmaceutical company. One of the ways we had decided to build engagement was by giving away some free samples of the product. This company was not well-known—not one of those with products you see on most drugstore shelves, but they did have some reach. Our goal was to build brand awareness for this product.

India is about nine hours ahead of most time zones in the States, so just before going to bed one night, I had a Skype conversation with my team back home. This was just before our planned kickoff for the contest we would use to give away free samples of this unique new product no one knew about. I went to bed thinking we would have moderate success—perhaps we would get a couple dozen people requesting it. After all, we weren't giving away Starbucks gift cards, and this was a unique product produced by a little known brand.

The next morning I awoke to find an emergency e-mail in my inbox: "Oh my gosh, Brian, it went viral! It got picked up by several very popular bloggers in the health industry, and not only did we blow through the thousands of samples we had (which we thought would last us months), but we 'oversold' free samples by 100 percent!" In one day, we had blown through the samples that should have lasted for months.

I then had the joy of calling the client to share the good news, that the campaign had wildly exceeded our expectations, and because we did not have a cap in place, we had given away more

@brianboyd

samples than we had in stock. The client was ecstatic and more than happy to fulfill all the sample requests.

What made this go viral? It is almost impossible to predict what will go viral, it just happens sometimes—and if you are on the receiving end, you are very fortunate. As much as I hate to admit it, as a consultant, part of it was just dumb luck. Still, we were able to pinpoint things that helped this contest go viral: great incentive, some great verbiage, a very clean landing page, and a connection with some very popular bloggers with big followings that made this thing blow up. (Notice the first three all had something to do with content.)

> The biggest blunder companies and organizations make with social media is talking about themselves all the time. It is the flagrant foul of the social media game.

Content-wise, the worst thing you can do is fail to generate a large quantity of it that is high quality. One of the cardinal rules of generating quality content is what we call the "MCP 70/30 Rule": Talk about others at least 70 percent of the time and talk about yourself less than 30 percent of the time. The biggest blunder companies and organizations make with social media is talking about themselves all the time. It is the flagrant foul of the social media game. No one wants to hear it—trust me.

A friend of mine, Deanna Zandt (@deanna), a consultant for the president's social media team and author of the book, *Share This! How You Will Change the World with Social Networking,* likens this to a party where you get stuck listening to a guy talk about himself the whole time. He drones on about how awesome he is, how awesome his kids are, his new car, how awesome his job is going, and so on. It isn't long before you are ready to walk away and move on to the next person. The only difference is, with social media, it is much easier to "walk away"—and walk away your followers and fans will. They may not necessarily stop following you, but they will stop paying attention and engaging.

Social media allows you to be the person at the party that asks others about themselves, where they're from, what they do for a living, what's going on in their job, and just generally shows interest in them and their lives. It allows you to interact and engage.

Make it your mission to talk at least 70 percent about competitors, clients, client success stories, your industry, news, what is happening in the world, trends, and so on. Talk 30 percent (or less) about your new products, your brand, your new book, your company, a new sales initiative, sales special, campaign, or fund-raiser—anything that contributes to your bottom line. If you mix it up like this—at least go into this mixing it up like this—the people who follow you will under-stand that your company truly cares for others. The MCP 70/30 Rule is simple, but it's amazing how some people still don't follow it.

Of course, if you use social media much, you will come across brands that do exactly the opposite of this. They spend every waking moment talking about themselves; and this is simply not an effective way to build rapport with customers, friends, and others who are watching them.

Social Media Content DO'S and DON'TS

Here are more rules and recommendations for generating great content:

- **DO be human.** Be honest and transparent. Canned, robotic efforts will not work. Balance being human with good sense. Recognize how you present yourself through social media.

- **DO commit time to social media.** Social media takes time. You cannot spend fifteen minutes a day on it and expect great results from your social media exercise.

- **DO post timely, relevant content.** Social media is all about immediate satisfaction. Your content must be about the latest and the greatest. If you do not capitalize on what's relevant, someone else will.

- **DO choose controversial, engaging content.** Choose content that gets people talking and that they can be passionate about.

- **DO mix it up.** Give your followers a variety of content so that each day they have a reason to visit your social media platforms to see what is going on. Post pictures, events, quotes, personal memes, articles, videos, and more.

- **DO strategize and keep an eye on your content...and be ready and willing to change.** What works today may not work tomorrow. You must be vigilant in watching which content does well and which doesn't. When it does not work, can it and switch to something that does.

- **DO engage.** Respond. Like. Answer. Show your audience you value their opinion and engage with them.

- **DO know your audience and what content does well.** Keep an eye on which content resonates with your audience and develop more of it. Measure *everything*.

- **DO watch "voice."** What do you sound like? What person do you speak in? Do you use too many exclamation points? Acronyms? Be careful with your voice.

- **DO make it personal.** Your followers and fans want to know it is you and not just a machine writing posts and responding.

- **DO respond in a timely manner.** Your customers expect a timely response to questions, comments, or concerns. Respond in four hours or less, if possible.

- **DON'T post without carefully thinking through and reviewing what you write.** Be sure to proofread your post and to test all links to be sure they work.

- **DON'T link your accounts.** Don't push out identical content on Facebook and Twitter.

- **DON'T delete negative comments.** Respond to them positively and courteously.

- **DON'T make it all personal.** No one wants to hear what you ate for breakfast.

- **DON'T let yourself get stagnant.** Social media changes constantly. Just because you have the winning recipe for social media content now does not mean you will still have it tomorrow.

- **DON'T sell.** This is not to say that you cannot promote things every once in a while, but no one wants to follow or buy from someone who constantly and only pushes some type of product or service.

- **DON'T get lazy.** Content has to be relevant and timely. Social media changes every day and you have to be on top of the game. For example, if you've written a book, do not always post quotes from it.

- **DON'T forget that social media is immediate and permanent.** Every word you write and post will be seen by millions in just a few seconds. And then it can live on forever. Think of what you post on the Internet as being written in ink—permanent.

Great Content Lives on Forever

Content will make or break your social media presence...and your brand. Great content can be unforgettable and have an incredibly lasting impact. On the infamous day of September 11, 2001 (9/11), I was in Lower Manhattan. I was one of the fortunate ones who knew my loved ones were okay and well away from the towers. I was also one of the fortunate ones as I, along with tens of thousands of other New Yorkers, fled from the vicinity of the falling towers. As I ran down the street, I would occasionally turn and take pictures. I don't know why. I think I just felt I needed to capture that "moment." At that point, none of us knew the extent of what was happening, and whether people had been killed or injured. It was just happening and we were watching...and running. It was a solemn, sad day...sad beyond words.

Later on, I posted several dozen very moving pictures I had taken in an album on Flickr (http://brianboyd.me), the popular social media photo sharing site. I have no security set on these images because I believe they belong to the world, so anyone can see them and share them. They have only creative commons licensing on them, so anyone can use them any way they want, whether on a blog or in a newspaper, as long as they show attribution and credit them properly. This also gave me the chance to share a little bit about our family, what we went through, and how thankful we are that God kept us safe, and that we do not take that for granted. Every year since then, on or around the anniversary of 9/11, this content becomes very popular. I receive tons of requests to use them and people leave comments on this social media platform, saying how moving the images are.

When it comes to content, this is what it is all about. I merely took some photos, posted them on a social media site, and tagged them to make them easy for people to find. Now, each year as we approach the anniversary of that unspeakably tragic day, these photos get used and reused countless times in blogs, magazines, newspapers, on Facebook pages, in tweets—all over the place.

At this writing, twelve years have passed and people on social media are still using these photographs on a regular basis to remind others of this tragedy. You never know the full impact of the content you put out on social media. The power of content should never be taken for granted or underestimated.

CHAPTER 6

Influence: Why You Need It and How to Get It

> "When E. F. Hutton talks...people listen."
> —E. F. Hutton ad campaign
>
> "Even fools are thought wise when they keep silent;
> with their mouths shut, they seem intelligent."
> —Proverbs 17:28 NLT

One of the most effective ad campaigns of the 80s was that of the stock brokerage firm, E. F. Hutton. In their classic commercials, someone in a crowded room would say, "E. F. Hutton says..." and the room would go silent. The voiceover would then intone: "When E. F. Hutton talks...people listen." The message was clear: E. F. Hutton was the voice of authority in their space. As a brand, they had incredible influence. There is something here for us today concerning influence and social media—though all influence is not equal and you may not find it where you expect it.

When we first engaged with a certain nonprofit client, they were fresh off a "pay to play" Twitter campaign with a famous athlete. (They had paid him a sizable sum to tweet support for them and the work they did.) Though this athlete had millions of followers, they received only a couple hundred clickthroughs on the link to their site in the tweet, and raised no money for their cause—not a dime. Why? It simply wasn't relevant to their audience. At our direction, they went on another platform and appealed to an audience that was closely aligned with their cause and received an 80 percent clickthrough rate and an impressive amount in donations.

My wife, Fran (@FranPaceBoyd), decided to run the New York City Marathon and, after Hurricane Sandy, she decided to run to raise funds for Samaritan's Purse (@SamaritansPurse). She pushed the news out to her social platforms and received quite a few donations because she has a loyal following and considerable influence. She had a friend in Los Angeles with many followers who pushed out the same message on social platforms and only one donation came in. Why? Followers of Fran's friend did not know Fran, and they were on the West Coast, far removed from Hurricane Sandy. Fran connected with the right kind of groups, the right kind of influence in the right geographical area and she raised a lot of money (much more than the aforementioned famous basketball player from California with millions of followers). When it comes to social media, don't be fooled by the big numbers. It is far better to spend your time focusing on the right audience and align with the right influencers.

What Is Influence and How Do You Get It?

You know you have social media influence when you make a statement, ask a question, or ask your audience to take some action and they do it—they engage. An influential blogger is not just one with a sizable following, but one who elicits a high percentage of engagement and action by followers and readers. So if you have 10,000 followers and at any point in time, 10 percent or so regularly engage and interact with you, you are far more influential than if you have 100,000 followers who never engage at all.

Influence can also vary, depending on platform. On Twitter, influence is measured by how many of your followers retweet or reply to your tweets. Influence on Facebook is measured in the number of shares, likes, and amount of interaction with your content. On LinkedIn, influence is measured by not just your number of connections but the number of endorsements, recommendations, and interaction with your relevant posts to groups. Every platform offers a unique way to build your influence and find aligned influencers.

So how do you build your influence? One large ministry we engaged with had this problem. Though they travel around the world filling stadiums, and have a wildly enthusiastic following, they had only around two million social media followers. Another ministry, a smaller one, had many more followers. Why? The larger ministry was failing to engage its followers and using the wrong approach to social media. They weren't growing their audience the right way, organically, by pushing out value—great content that gets reposted and gets people talking about them and their content, developing both relationship and engagement. Another key way to build influence is to align with influencers who share your demographic.

How to Find Influencers

Your brand has stories to share. Every brand does. And these stories provide a vital link with influencers. Yours may be stories about your company or its products, but no matter what you're trying to share, your stories will resonate far better with people who are aligned with your thoughts, beliefs, and interests. And if these people have large, engaged followings, they are influencers.

Not long ago, I flew to California to meet with a major international organization in the fitness industry (a front of mind organization for everyone in the fitness industry). I spoke with one of the executives who told me they had no problem reaching their own followers, but they just needed more people to hear about them. So this was the key challenge: reaching new eyeballs by connecting with influencers. They are not alone. When clients first engage with us, the number one challenge most want to talk about is how to connect with influencers and reach new eyeballs. It is likely your company or organization faces this challenge as well.

The good news is, there are a number of ways to engage with influencers. Search.twitter.com is a great simple tool for finding Twitter users that are aligned and have interests similar to yours and those of your company. In 2013, Facebook released Graph Search, another great tool for finding influencers, allowing you to easily search for friends and others with similar interests. Some are better than others, but every platform offers a pathway to find influencers.

Michael Wu has written, "This topic is so deep and important that people start companies (e.g., Klout) just to find the influencers." Wu makes a good point, though I believe there are two relatively easy steps organizations and companies can take to find and engage with influencers (short of starting of a new company): Look inside your own company and engage with bloggers.

Look Inside Your Company

Many companies and organizations forget that their staff members, the people who work for them, are the first place to look for influencers. These are people who already believe in you, believe in the company and the brand, and have a vested interest in its success. Undoubtedly, they are already talking about where they work and the things they are involved in. This makes them the perfect first place to look for influencers.

One client of ours in Atlanta is in the retail space. We had the opportunity to set up their initial public facing social media sites for Facebook, Twitter, LinkedIn, and YouTube. The company had hundreds of employees, fertile ground for finding influencers—or so we thought. After launching the pages, we were surprised to find that only a handful of employees had even liked the pages. It was amazing to us that the vast majority did not engage on the company's social media sites. All possible conclusions we drew from this were troubling:

A) They didn't like their company,

B) They didn't understand how their engagement could help their company succeed (or how this was good for them), or

C) Their management and supervisory team had failed to sell them on engaging with the company on its social media pages.

Imagine you were a company with 500 employees and each of them liked your pages and shared one article a week. Noodle on the math of this and think of how many people your pages could reach. If each of your employees has 200 friends on Facebook, and each shares one article a week on Facebook, that article would reach 100,000 potential eyeballs. This is very exciting. If your organization is a nonprofit in the business of disaster relief, imagine the incredible potential for reaching new and existing donors if each of your employees shared a success story of how your organization fed an entire village, helped a family build a home, or provided medical care to children. The potential is limitless.

One of the richest sources for influencers is your very own staff. Though without exception, every client we have engaged were simply not doing this. They had overlooked the mass of potential for influencers within their own company. Make sure your employees know the power of what they do on social media, the potential benefits to the company (and themselves) for engaging with the company social media sites, and encourage them to be influencers for you. At Media Connect Partners (MCP), we include engagement with the company social media pages in every job description. It is an expectation for every employee. You would be wise to do this as well.

Engage with Bloggers

Hopefully, you are doing a great job talking to your existing audience through social media, your e-mail lists, your Facebook friends, your Twitter followers, but undoubtedly you want to reach new eyeballs. This whole exercise—engaging with bloggers—is about finding new eyeballs; people who are aligned with your beliefs and business but do not know about you. To engage with even one blogger with thousands of followers is a huge deal.

Step 1—Find Them

Use blogger directories and the major search engines to find bloggers who write on topics that are aligned with those of your organization (those in your vertical). Pull a list of the top twenty or fifty such bloggers. If your organization is in the health food industry, and you find an influential blogger who writes about healthy diets and eating habits, what do you do first?

Step 2—Interact with Them

Start following them. Connect with them on LinkedIn. Retweet them. Repost their content. Share their Facebook posts. Show that you are interested in their content. Over time, they will take notice of you or your company.

Step 3—Reach Out to Them

Reach out to the influencers to let them know about your organization or company, and that you are in the same industry (or how you are aligned). Keep in mind that influential bloggers get tons of requests, even hundreds a day, from those who wish to leverage their influence to build their brands. Simply e-mailing them a hello is not going to do the job. You must approach them with something to offer. One of the best things you can offer is quality content. Let them know you would love to guest blog for them or have them guest blog for you. Such a guest blog tradeoff is huge, and can present a major opportunity for your brand to reach a new audience.

Reaching Out to Trisha Novotny

A few years ago, a good friend of mine in the Seattle area, Trisha Novotny (@247moms), founded the blog *24/7 Moms* (http://247moms.com/), dedicated to providing information, help, and tips every family needs: healthy eating, where to get stuff on sale, recipes, topics for families to discuss around the dinner table, and much more. The blog is wildly popular and Trisha gets an incredible number of views and visits on all her social platforms. It is no surprise that she also gets hundreds of requests a day from people who want to get on her blog to gain the benefits of her influence for their own brand. Again, simply e-mailing big-time influencers like Trisha will not grab their attention or elicit a response. So how do you position yourself to merit their support or help?

If you are part of the health food industry organization mentioned earlier, and you want to get on the radar of a great influencer like Trisha who aligns with your industry, you need to connect with her on LinkedIn, start engaging with her in the comment section of her blog, repost her Facebook posts, retweet her tweets, and share her videos. After doing this for some time, she will get to know who you are, and then you can go in and ask for a favor.

For example, offer a guest blogging opportunity. Approach Trisha and say, "Hey, I would love to have you guest blog for us." Given the industry alignment, familiarity with you, and the opportunity for her to potentially reach many new eyeballs, it is likely she will be very happy to guest post. By her merely blogging for you, it guarantees you will reach many new eyeballs as well (and gives your blogger a day off).

Obstacles to Overcome

In the context of discussing influencers in social media with clients, I've noticed they can run into three mental obstacles:

1) **Impatience**—How can I get influence fast—like yesterday?

2) **Influence Inequality**—How can I engage with and work with an influencer who has greater influence than me?

3) **Competition**—What if I sense the influencers I want to engage are competitive to my brand?

In answer to the first obstacle, influence inequality, you need not be equal in influence for your brand to be attractive to influencers. For example, even if you are part of a recently launched very small magazine seeking a foothold in the mommy blogger marketplace, you have something to offer—you have content, and content is what influencers need to give their audience. You may not have the hundreds of thousands of followers that are influencers like *24/7 Moms* does, but you do have something they can use, something they need: content. You could also offer them giveaways or prizes—be creative.

In response to the second obstacle, competition, I simply acknowledge the sense of competition is out there to some degree, but anyone with their head screwed on straight in the social media space understands that the whole idea of social media is to engage and build relationships. Stay away from a combative, competitive attitude. These will seriously hinder your social media efforts. If you face it from influencers, simply move on to others who get social media and play well with others.

In response to the third obstacle, if your brand wants to be influential, there is no quick, secret, or magical way to gain it, particularly if your brand is new to social media. This goes back to what we've covered: You need to create consistent quality content, push it out across platforms on a regular basis, engage your audience, engage other influencers, and stay true to that task.

Over time, you will become a true influencer in your category as well. Give it a year or two. It won't happen overnight.

Maintaining Your Influence— Continual Cliffhangers

Once you have influence, how do you keep it? The number one key for maintaining one's influence is to keep pushing out consistently good content at a rate your audience values. There is no scientific method to how much to share and how often to share it. The balance is tricky, but wise brands pay close attention to this. People tend to tune out companies and organizations that overshare. Understand, there is a fine line between keeping your audience engaged and boring them. Keep them on the edge of their seats. Produce cliffhanger content.

My wife, Fran, doesn't talk a whole lot on social media. In fact, she shares very infrequently. She prefers to listen a lot. However, when she does share, she gets an enormous amount of interaction. The number of those who comment, like, share, and otherwise interact with her content is staggering. I think this goes back to the E. F. Hutton idea. She doesn't overshare or overdo it with interaction, her audience is closely aligned with her, and she is transparent, so when she does push something out through her sphere of influence, people pay attention to it.

At MCP, we evaluate this on a case-by-case basis. There are many factors to weigh in deciding what is too much: what you do, what kind of brand you are, and the people you are talking to. This is an area where your friends and followers can serve you well as a focus group. Ask them: "Hey, are we talking too much? Are we pushing out too much content?" The ultimate key to maintaining your influence is to keep your audience engaged without losing them or boring them.

Convert Your Audience to Influencers

Whenever I meet with companies, I always make the point (or remind them) that social media makes for great focus groups, providing an excellent environment for getting quality feedback fast, *if* you are engaged well with your audience and have built trust with them. This always seems to be an "aha!" Now it won't be for you!

Your social media presence provides you with an audience that is interested in your brand, what you have to say, your advice, what you have to sell, and what you represent. It also offers you a focus group you can turn to for help or to ask questions. By allowing them to have a say in what you decide, it empowers them and makes them feel valued.

Recently, a celebrity asked her social media audience what she should wear on the red carpet for a special event. Another asked which color nail polish she should wear to an event. An author might tweet or post: "I am writing a book about _____, so what should my Chapter 10 be?" As a brand, when you need to make a strategic decision, through social media you can ask your audience to weigh in and take part in making that decision. Of course, when they do, remember to thank them by giving them a shout-out on social media. No matter what you may think or hear others say, people like to have their names in lights. Besides, this is just part of being social.

When *Prevention* magazine used social media to elicit questions from fans and followers to drive editorial content, they recognized and thanked those whose ideas they had used right there in the pages of the magazine itself. So if Judy from Wisconsin gave them an idea that made a great point for an article, they gave her a shout-out in print. This was meaningful to her and helped build their stature as a relational brand that cares about its audience.

@brianboyd

Reminder: It's Not a Numbers Game

One of our mantras at MCP is, "It's not a numbers game." Social media success and growth are not found solely in the number of followers, likes, or members of your network. You don't need to have more followers than anyone else to have a successful social media practice. It's about getting the right kind of followers, quality engagement with them, and getting influencers involved. You want to connect with people who connect with you.

At the end of the day, everyone has influence. There is a joke in my house that whenever I get together with friends, I make them spend money. I am usually the guy who gets asked about new gadgets and electronics. For example, I'm the guy who gets real excited about that new device, say, that charges your iPhone three times as fast as normal and only costs $14 on Amazon. I am up on all this stuff and when I talk about things like this, people buy them. Don't get blinded by the big numbers of followers and fans other brands have. You are influential. I am influential. So are others right around you. Our focus should be on using our influence well and growing it through quality engagement with our audience and alignment with key influencers.

CHAPTER 7

Building the Relationship (Measuring your ROR— Return on Relationship)

"You can't have influence if you don't build a relationship."
—Lisa Boshoff

Not long ago, I was in South Africa to speak to a group of 150 CEOs and executives about social media. We were fortunate to have drivers assigned to us each day to get us anywhere we needed to go. (This was to ensure the safety of the South African people. They wouldn't have wanted to risk me driving on the "wrong" side of the road.) One day, our driver was a young woman named Lisa Boshoff. Lisa works for the faith-based organization, Doxa Deo, in Pretoria (http://www.doxadeo.co.za). She runs an outreach of the church, working with youth in the public schools. She talked about how the church was working in the school system.

"We're trying to get in there and engage with these kids and teach them about life, priorities, making smart choices, and more," she said.

"How exactly do you do that?" I asked.

"Well, it's really important to us that we build relationships with these young people, because as a church organization, we know that we'll never have influence without relationship."

> We'll never have influence in social media without relationship.

What she said was so good, I created a slide for it and added it to my presentation. Highlight this: We'll never have influence in social media without relationship. Whether you're a physical therapy association, a church, or a retail store that sells art and craft supplies, your social media campaign focus should be to build relationships. Telling your story works with relationships.

Every Company Has a Story: Tell Yours

We just booked a trip to Kolkata, India. We will be working with the Assembly of God church (http://www.agkolkata.org), building their marketing and social strategies. Through their Kolkata Mission, they run a hospital, feed 25,000 people a day, and provide free medical care to 40,000 people annually. They work with local people to educate them and teach them skill sets they need to find work and support themselves. Working with so many people, surely they have countless stories to tell of those they feed and care for. By so doing, they also tell the story of the Mission.

A South African organization, POPUP (The People Upliftment Programme, http://www.popup.co.za), provides skills development and training for unemployed and disempowered individuals, and also manages social support services. One of their students came in off the street, attended and graduated from their culinary school, and did so well that he was hired by the Sheraton in Johannesburg, a five-star hotel, where he now serves as one of their senior chefs. A local newspaper even published a story about him. This is a great story to share.

Both the Kolkata Mission and POPUP are doing incredible work and have phenomenal stories to share. When you are feeding 25,000 people a day or teaching people skills that equip them to make a dramatic turnaround in their life, you will have any number of amazing stories to tell. However, you must tell them. Your company or organization has great stories to share as well. The question is, are you sharing them? Most companies forget to do this.

> There is no better way to attract a new audience than this: Tell a story—tell *your* story.

As a brand, if you are not actively looking for stories and pushing them out on social media consistently, you are missing a great opportunity to engage your existing audience and attract new audiences. The majority of your social media time budget should be invested in looking for great content and stories, and less about aimless activity (like frequently posting random thoughts on Twitter). There is no better way to attract a new audience than this: Tell a story—tell *your* story.

Your existing audience is made up of your current customers, subscribers, partners, donors, fans, and others who are engaged with you. There is great value to your brand in keeping this audience abreast of what is happening in your organization. But it's just not enough to engage your current audience all the time. If you have 10,000 likes on Facebook, it's easy to come up with content just for them. To stop there is shortsighted and simply not good enough if you hope to grow your business through social media. You need a plan for engaging new audiences.

To attract new members to your audience, you have to make your brand stand out from the crowd. Nothing does this better than pushing out content on social media that tells your story in a compelling, memorable way. So part of your plan for attracting new eyeballs and new audiences should involve thinking through the content you have and the stories you can share, using them to engage and begin relationships, and injecting them into numerous mediums. And you must do this with an eye to make the content easily shareable through social media platforms. If these new audiences turn to share content with others, you can grow your brand exponentially.

Guest blogging is a great tactic for finding new audiences. As a guest blogger, you provide your host with something of great value to them (content), and they provide you with something of great value, an opportunity to share your story (new information) with a new audience. It's a win-win. For instance, if you are a blogger for the Assembly of God church in Kolkata, the organization that does such an amazing outreach to people in need every day, you should be looking at other blogs around the world for potential guest blogging opportunities.

> If you fail to tell your brand's story,
> it could become the best story *never* told.

Never forget this: Tell a story—tell your story. If you fail to tell your brand's story, it could become the best story *never* told.

Don't Let Yours Be the Best Story Never Told

I am fortunate that my business takes me all over the world. I've enjoyed the opportunity to meet with a number of fascinating companies and organizations. The problem is, in many cases I had no idea of their incredible work or story until I was on site with them. There was little or nothing to be found on social media. This was our experience most recently in South Africa.

Prior to traveling to South Africa, Fran and I had done quite a bit of research on where we were going. Still, when we got there, we had little to no idea what was happening with many of the organizations we visited. A number of times, Fran and I looked over at each other and mouthed, "I had no idea." I remember telling our hosts: "Wait a minute, guys. I had no idea you were doing this stuff!"

At one organization's offices, I opened the door and saw dozens of computers and Microsoft Office signs on the wall. They were teaching Microsoft Excel to people in need of marketable work skills, and many of them were at risk of becoming homeless. Many of them had no other personal access to this technology or training. Each of the people this organization helps is initially given a placement exam to guide them to a good vocational match, whether business management, office work, computer programming, sewing and fabrics, culinary arts, or others. Then the organization trains them in their vocation.

I looked over one woman's shoulder and saw she was working on a complex Excel spreadsheet. (Excel can be challenging, and I know that many people consider it very difficult to teach or understand.) As I watched, this woman and others were manipulating spreadsheets like master Excel experts. I loved the philosophy behind this organization's work, the proverbial principle: "Give a man a fish and you feed him for a day. Teach a man to fish and you feed him for a lifetime." There are plenty of organizations with soup kitchens and feeding lines, but this organization educates men and women so they can reenter the workforce, contribute to society, and do many cool things. This organization had countless success stories to tell of men and women who had finished their program, entered the workforce, and had their lives turned around. I had no idea this was happening. They were a well-kept secret, a story not being told.

We had to go all the way to Johannesburg and tour a number of these organizations and companies in person to learn about all the amazing things they were doing, to hear their stories. We should have been able to understand and genuinely capture the depth of what they were doing and the impact they were making in South Africa from anywhere in the world. Theirs are some of the best stories never being told. They need to be told, and social media is perfect for this. Through it, these organizations are able to tell the world what is different about them—what sets them apart from the crowd.

> As an executive, ask yourself if your brand is telling your story so effectively that anywhere in the world, people can understand what you're about and grasp the impact you're having in the business world.
>
> You're not doing your organization any favors by not telling the world your story.

As an executive, ask yourself if your brand is telling your story so effectively that anywhere in the world, people can understand what you're about and grasp the impact you're having in the business world. Your organization is making an impact. Do people know about it? If not, understand that you're not doing your organization any favors by not telling the world your story.

No matter what your business is, whether publishing, gardening, faith, nonprofit, or selling men's face cream, are you telling your story so often and well that I feel invested in your brand, part of the family, in relationship with it? Your team must think this through. This is another little filter that you as an executive should look at to be sure your team is getting the job done, telling your story. We bootstrapped Media Connect Partners from the ground up, with tons of stories along the way. We constantly challenge ourselves to do a better job at telling our story.

Social Media Fit for the B-to-B Organization

"We're a B-to-B organization (business-to-business, a business that sells to or serves other businesses). Is social media a good fit for us?" We get asked this question quite often. I immediately respond, "You bet!" Because if you are a B-to-B organization, you know who your target is. If you create and sell screws, you know that hardware stores, Home Depot, Lowes, and others are your target. As a B-to-B, when you know who your target is, you can actually reach out and target blogs that are fully into your product and seek other connections through various social media platforms. In this regard, it makes more sense for B-to-B brands to use social media than it would for B-to-C organizations (business-to-consumer). It is far more difficult to reach all the consumers in North America with your end product (as B-to-C brands must do) because you hit hundreds of millions of nonaligned and potentially uninterested consumers with your message. It is a much more difficult engagement. Social media is important to B-to-B brands and proven to be a great opportunity for Media Connect Partners.

One of our clients, Hobby Lobby, has source materials from companies that make things like fabric, wood, and many others that people use in arts and crafts. Their suppliers, no matter where they are in the world, are all looking for that B-to-B exchange. If I'm a buyer at Hobby Lobby, and I'm looking for a certain kind of item, say burlap, I may go online and look for burlap manufacturers. The odds are that the top burlap manufacturer to catch my eye online is the one that has done the best job executing a quality social media and online marketing campaign that told their story well and got them noticed.

To be that burlap manufacturer that gets noticed, ideally, I would create a regular blog and social media presence, and work on search engine optimization around my website. I would create a social media campaign where I talk about: how burlap is such a trendy fabric, why our burlap is the best, the many things that can be done with burlap, what our customers are saying about burlap, the creative ways they are using it, and more. Then I would thoroughly infiltrate all the online social media platforms so that when anybody is searching for burlap, I will come up in searches and be represented. (This is key.) As a B-to-B provider, I would then know who my target is. Then I can actually reach out to blogs that are related to my product, and engage with key influencers who will talk about my product a lot. I can reach out to conferences that have social media around them, to gain visibility there. I can align myself with certain Twitter hashtags (as these filter content and serve as a pseudo index of Twitter), so I can easily find tweets and listen in.

Recently, a friend of mine posted a screenshot on Instagram of a certain product she had purchased. She used the product's name in the photo description. The company that sold the product was "listening," actively monitoring use of their name in postings online. They found their name being used and commented on her Instagram photo: "Hey, thank you so much for using our product. We're excited that you're a customer. If there is anything we can do, let us know!" Of course, this impressed her and made her feel a part of the brand's "family," so she shared it with many people— exactly what the brand hoped she would do.

Listening is the key for making any human relationship grow and develop, but it is also essential for the growth and development of social media relationships. There are many ways to "listen" on the Internet and find discussions about your brand or industry online. Then you can target those who participate in these discussions to engage with them and establish or build relationships. Every B-to-B organization should set up listening campaigns, using key tools. There are a number of them.

Social Media Listening Tools

Google News Alerts

This is the most obvious listening tool. Set up news alerts with key words. If your business is in fabric, burlap, or fashion trends, set these up as alerts in your Google account (i.e., "fabric," "burlap," "fashion trends"). Then, when someone "talks" about those key words online, whether in tweets, blog posts, Facebook posts, and more, Google will alert you via e-mail and you can listen in and easily interact with the talkers.

Facebook Insights

With the advent of Insights, Facebook created an intelligent system that allows brand managers to develop actionable data around their digital footprint.

TweetStats

(http://tweetstats.com)

Use this to monitor:

- Tweets per hour
- Tweets per month
- Tweet timeline
- Reply statistics

Statigram

(http://statigram.com)

Statigram connects to Instagram and provides charts and graphs that allow you to analyze your account and actions.

Radian6

(http://www.salesforcemarketingcloud.com/)

This listening device allows companies to filter what is being said about their brand online so they can engage users.

Sprout Social

(http://sproutsocial.com)

Use this to monitor and track your brand across various social media sites: Twitter, Facebook, Foursquare, LinkedIn, and Yelp.

Trendrr

(http://trendrr.tv)

Trendrr measures social media activity related to specific television shows (e.g., mentions, likes, check-ins) across Twitter, Facebook, GetGlue, and Viggle.

Listening Tools to Determine Key Social Influencers

Klout

(http://klout.com)

Klout is a measuring tool that illustrates the amount of influence a typical user or brand has across their various social media profiles, including: Twitter, Facebook, Foursquare, YouTube, Instagram, and Google.

PeerIndex

(http://peerindex.com)

PeerIndex gives you point system analysis of your social grid. It combines the ideas of Klout, while giving you discounts and perks from online retailers.

@brianboyd

Kred

(http://kred.com)

Kred assigns scores to users based on their influence and outreach on Twitter, Facebook, and LinkedIn.

FollowerWonk

(http://followerwonk.com)

FollowerWonk breaks out follower value based on authority.

The ROR Funnel

In an earlier chapter, I made the point that a brand's social media success should be measured in conversion, and that sales, donations, or whatever you define as conversion, are part of ROR (return on relationship). The whole idea for social media is relationships. You engage in social media as a brand. You tell your story, you put out great content, you follow the 70/30 rule, and you become a thought leader in your space. As people all around the world start engaging with you, you engage back, and you begin to build relationships with them. So far, so good, but ideally you don't leave it there. The key to ROR is driving these relationships down the ROR funnel (see it above) to your blog, website, or 800 number, where you can make a conversion.

This funnel always seems to get a lot of traction with executives and sales leaders. This was true again in a recent sales meeting as I presented what we do to a new client. They latched onto the fact that they must try to build relationships and keep them in social media where they get initial engagement. They must push out initial content and get some feedback. Then they must start a conversation and respond when people ask questions. As they talk to people and become friends, these friends will turn and share with their friends. All this works together to drive these relationships down the ROR funnel to their blog, website, or 800 number.

Why is it important to drive them down through the ROR funnel to your blog, website, or 800 number? This will give you better control over the relationship. After all, your business does not exist to make money for Facebook, Twitter, or any other social platform. If your relationships stall at the social media platform level, say Facebook, it is Facebook's gain, not yours. They own that platform, you don't. So you drive the relationship down to where they engage with you on your website or blog, platforms you own and control. You have more control over converting that person however you want to convert them—to a buyer, donor, e-mail or mailing list contact, 800 number caller—whatever conversion you need. The end goal is driving them down the funnel to conversion.

It seems that many brands focus on leaving people in the top area of the funnel—up in the social media platforms. This is fine for a time, but eventually they must seek to engage their likes and followers on a deeper level, and convert them there.

Recently, we ran a contest on Facebook for a client. Over the course of two weeks, we gathered over 100,000 e-mail addresses of people who wanted to enter the contest. This was great for the contest, but more important, those e-mail addresses were added to the client's e-mail marketing software, so they could continue to dialogue, keep the relationship up, and engage them. Not all of these e-mail addresses will stick, some will opt out and that's fine. (We all want to play by the rules. No one wants to be a spammer.) But the fact is, we converted them from social media to the client's own website: 100,000 conversions (opt-ins for the e-mail marketing list).

Think of how many followers, fans, and friends you have on Facebook, YouTube, and Twitter. You cannot manage them because you do not own them as long as they remain there. You must move them down through the funnel. You don't know what tomorrow holds for these platforms—no one does. In social media, it is hard for anyone to see even six months ahead. These platforms might change dramatically or even be gone tomorrow, replaced by something else (see MySpace and Google Buzz). You have no control over these platforms or how they manage you and your followers, friends, and likes. This should serve as a strong motivation for you to move them down through the funnel, to the platforms you own, manage, and control. You must have a solid, long-term vision for moving people to the place where you engage them—your blog, for instance. There are plenty of stories of people who have built successful businesses off blogs. They control their blog and that is why they are so successful.

Every year, Joel Osteen holds large stadium events called America's Night of Hope (http://AmericasNightOfHope.com). Basically, Joel takes Lakewood Church on the road, music, worship and all, and he delivers a message. At the end of the evening, he asks everyone in the stadium, usually around 40,000 people, to stand if the event had an impact on them, caused them to make a decision, or if they simply need prayer. He tells everyone else to reach out to those standing, and they are each given cards to fill out.

As they do this in the stadium, Media Connect Partners engages with those participating through social media. Every year, for these stadium events, we produce a live event online, using streaming media, live Twitter, live Facebook, and interactive chat where we talk with everyone in the social audience. When Joel asks everyone in the stadium to stand, we ask everyone online to stand too, literally, right there in front of their computer or whatever. We've had thousands and thousands of people stand up, typing in the chat room, "I'm standing." This happened because we spent a lot of time building relationships over the course of the weeks prior to the event and engaged with the audience during the event itself. We talked with them, answered their questions, made sure they were enjoying the event, followed along, interacted, and so on. So at the end of the night, when Joel led the stand up moment, they were invested.

After they indicated they had stood, we sent them to an URL that directed them to a landing page where they could enter contact information similar to what those in the stadium wrote on cards. Afterward, Lakewood Church followed up on all these contacts, connecting them with a local church.

That stand up moment isn't about somebody buying something, making a donation, or even opting in to something. But it is a conversion valued by Lakewood Church, and genuine return on relationship (ROR). When conversion happens, it is always amazing.

CHAPTER 8

Creating a Solid Social Media Strategy

> "How can you squander even one more day not taking advantage of the greatest shifts of our generation? How dare you settle for less when the world has made it so easy for you to be remarkable?"
>
> —Seth Godin

Some time ago, we were flown in to meet with some executives and the marketing team for a well-known brick-and-mortar organization that sells "widgets" in many regions of the U.S. (I'm being purposefully vague here.) When we prompted these executives, "Hey, let's talk about your existing social media strategy," not only did they express that they did not have one, but we found that the young woman they had put in charge of pushing out content on social media for the last year and a half had been given very little direction at all. When I asked her to produce all the analytics so we could see where they were, where they had come from, and how well they had been doing, she couldn't produce anything. Nothing. She had no clue. Flustered, she looked across the table at us and said, "We know we really get this demographic." When I asked how she knew this, she said, "Because we're in our mid-twenties, we're not old."

In fact, the brand had entrusted their social voice to someone who basically had no training and no direction for what was most important to say about their brand to the world. This company would never, not in a million years, dare to air a TV commercial without some sort of structure, platform, plan, or branded message. An architect wouldn't think of building a building without a plan or a strategy. Yet, here they were, communicating with potentially millions of people, and entrusting it to a novice with no clear plan.

Brands seem to forget all about creating a solid social media plan. They just get out there and start tweeting! Perhaps they do not realize what they are doing, or no one has taught them, but this is critical. We've found that very few brands have a written, formal social media strategy.

When we begin to engage with a brand, whether they are a big established brand or a small brand, we ask, "Can you please send us your formal, written social media strategy?" They typically respond, with few exceptions: "We don't have one." Many brands will have a written, formalized branding design guide that dictates in strict terms how their logo should appear (typeface, colors, etc.). They will have a formal, written style guide. They will have a variety of written, formalized human resources policies. They will even have a written, formalized communication plan or acceptable use policy for employees. Yet they do not have a written, formalized social media strategy—how they plan to communicate their brand *to the world*.

Think back to the South African organizations mentioned in the previous chapter that are educating hundreds of South Africans on a regular basis, teaching them skills so they can go and make a difference in the working world. Theirs is a great story to tell on social media. Imagine what would happen if someone without training, without direction, messed up their story and turned it on its knees because they weren't trained correctly. What if they put out a tweet that offended a group you had hoped to attract? What if they posted something with profanity in it due to a typo? What if they posted generally poor posts so often that your brand began losing fans and followers? All this could be devastating for your business, even causing your bottom line (P&L) to bottom out. Already this year we've seen a couple of major brands hacked online, causing stock prices to swing. What you say on social media and how you say it all needs to be in your formal, written social media strategy.

It is hard for me not to be nervous and a bit passionate about this with clients. It's time to get it done. You can't skate by anymore. It's a big deal. Time's up.

That's where we come in, to walk them through a tried and true process we've used successfully many times to help our clients create their written, formal social media strategy. It's a fun time because it puts the organization through a valuable exercise in which they think through what they're saying to the world and how they say it. At the end of the process, we give them their complete social media strategy (usually about sixty pages long, but easy to follow). In this chapter, I'll walk through some of the process we use.

Step 1—Diversify Your Approach

The first thing we do is help the organization think about the approach, specifically about taking a diversified approach. One group called us recently and asked why we were more expensive than a consultant they were working with.

"What are they doing for you?" I asked, in order to begin an apples to apples comparison.

They outlined a number of things the consultant had done for them on Facebook. "They did X on Facebook, they did Y on Facebook, and they did Z on Facebook." Then they shared the results they knew of from this "Facebook only" strategy. They were underwhelmed by the results, as was I.

"I see the problem," I said.

"What?"

"They're building you a Facebook strategy. Facebook is making a lot of money, but you're not."

"Um, yeah."

"Do you have a comprehensive, diverse social strategy?"

"No."

I went on to tell them that we weren't in business to make Facebook, Twitter, or any other platform money—nor should they be. We were in business to make them, the brand, money.

Don't make the mistake this brand and this consultant made. Don't focus all your efforts on one platform. Be diversified in your approach—think about it all: your website, your blog, Facebook, Twitter, YouTube, Wikipedia, LinkedIn, and so on. You need to think about all of these. If you aren't somewhere in all of these platforms, you are probably missing opportunities to engage with an existing or brand-new audience. The first thing you need to do is think in terms of a diversified approach.

Step 2—Talk to *Your* Audience

Once you have diversified your approach across platforms, you must think about the diversified audience. Are you a B-to-B organization or a B-to-C organization? How you talk is going to differ depending on who you are trying to reach. What you say, the way you say it, and the tactics that come later on in this chapter are going to differ depending on whom you are trying to reach.

Step 3—Manage Your Social SEO

One huge reason it is so important to have a strategy is that your social media connections will correlate directly with how well you are seen online and whether or not you are noticed there—how you come up in searches. For example, in 2013, Facebook created an upgrade to their search algorithm called Facebook Graph Search. It replaced the search box in Facebook. It also propagated to other search engines, including Google, Bing, and Yahoo.

@brianboyd

It works like this. Say your name is Sam and you live near Briny Breezes, Florida, as does your Facebook friend, Greg. Greg has made it known on Facebook that he loves hot wings, especially those from his favorite restaurant, Blazing Saddles Hot Wings, in Briny Breezes, Florida. So when you type, "Hey, who has the best hot wings?" in Facebook, behind the scenes, in seconds, Facebook gets to work. Sam is friends with Greg. Greg likes hot wings, especially those from Blazing Saddles Hot Wings, in Briny Breezes, Florida. Sam is looking for the best hot wings, and he will probably like the ones his friend, Greg, likes. Then it pushes you a list of places where you should eat and why they are good, with Blazing Saddles Hot Wings right at the top. The first result will be something that social media (in this case, Facebook) believes you'll like because of your connections. So, if you are Blazing Saddles Hot Wings, in Briny Breezes, Florida, you want to engage in social media with as many connections as possible so that when people are looking for the best hot wings, you will come up high in the results. You are there. *You won't be there without engaging in social media.*

We are seeing it more and more: Brands with social connections succeed. So if you're a brand and you've spent time building these social connections, you will have success in business, in marketing—all over. If you don't have social connections and do not engage through social media, you will be invisible because traditional SEO is morphing into social SEO.

Step 4—Refine *Your* Voice

Recently, we met with an organization that said they were trying to reach the teen demographic, those thirteen to eighteen years old. Yet as we evaluated their social media messages, they sounded as if they were in their fifties. Their voice was all wrong.

In Chapter 5, I covered the importance of consistently pushing out high quality content to social media success, but it is also important to understand the importance of your social media voice. To refine your voice, get your marketing and communications team together, gather them around a whiteboard (blackboard, or big sheet of paper), keep them away from computers and phones, and list out the characteristics of your desired voice. Write down as many descriptors as you can. This progression should help guide your discussion:

- **Describe our current social media "voice." What do we sound like?**
- **What do we want to sound like?**

  Do we want to sound authentic? Do we want to sound professional? Do we want to sound youthful? Do we want to sound hip? Do we want to use acronyms—OMG, LOL, ROFL, ROTFLOL (rolling on the floor laughing out loud)? Do we want to speak in first person or third person? Do we want to use few exclamation points?

- **In light of all we've written here, let's boil down our desired voice to the ten most important characteristics. What are they?** (You need not come up with exactly ten. You might come up with more or less.)

As I read the posts that come out of your organization, I should be able to discern these characteristics in every one. Every post that does not match with these characteristics should be rewritten. My recommendation is that this list of characteristics be adjacent to the computer used by whoever is writing your content, as a filter they must use to make sure every post matches the characteristics.

Many times, instead of a brand's posts sounding like their voice, they sound like the voice of the person writing them. You can go to the social media of some stores online and say: "That sounds like a young lady," or "That sounds like a young man," or "That sounds like an activist with an axe to grind" (the latter would not be good for the brand trying for the "feel-good" voice characteristic). You can tell who is writing based on the way it sounds, which should be secondary to the brand's voice (if there at all).

> Your brand needs a voice that accurately conveys your brand identity.

Your brand needs a voice that accurately conveys your brand identity. Everything you do in social media must echo the list of characteristics you've identified that will foster your brand's voice and identity.

Step 5—Itemize Your Goals

The next thing to do is itemize the goals you have as an organization, and then plot the strategies and tactics you can use to meet them. To do this, gather the same group of people you met with earlier and get them back in front of the whiteboard and work together to list your top 15-20 goals as an organization. Keep in mind, you aren't even talking about social media yet, nor marketing goals. You are talking about your organization's top goals, whatever they may be: build our e-mail database, have more influence in our area or region, enter a new demographic, sell more widgets, make an impact on a community, improve our sentiment rating, and so on.

Next, see if you can put these goals into three or four smaller buckets. Do some of the goals have similar outcomes or ROI? For instance, do several relate to selling widgets, or perhaps driving website visits? Try to combine them together. Begin to fashion a hierarchy on the whiteboard by listing the top goals across the top. If you can put them into three or four buckets, that would be ideal.

Then drill down into your goals, listing beneath each one how you will measure success in reaching it. For example, if your goal is to build your e-mail database, how would you measure it? You would measure it by the number of opt-ins on your e-mail list. You can easily see if your numbers are going up or down, and if subscribers are increasing or not. This is an easy one. Now, if your goal is to have an impact on the Chicagoland area, then these two could actually work together because you can see who from the Chicagoland area is signing up for a specific e-mail campaign.

After you have determined how to measure the success of each goal, it is time to add tactics below them. This is also where you apply social media. Which social media tactics can you deploy to meet each goal? For example, one tactic to build your e-mail list database could be a contest on Facebook where you give away something like a set of DVDs. To enter the contest, people would have to give their e-mail address, their city, state, and zip code, and opt-in to join your list. Notice what's happened. You have met your goal because you've acquired subscribers to your mailing list, and by collecting their demographic information you know which part of the country they are in. This can determine how well you've met your other goal, making an impact on the Chicagoland area.

Another tactic would be a geo-targeting. For instance, Foursquare, Facebook, and even LinkedIn allow you to target posts and ads to a certain part of the country. Given our example above, you can target people in the Chicagoland area with your contest, saying, "Listen up, Chicagoland, we're running a contest. Enter here to sign up!" So this is a specific tactic you can use to meet your goal.

A third tactic for reaching the Chicagoland area would be engaging with bloggers in that part of the country. Deploy a member of your team to research bloggers in your category in the Chicagoland area that you can engage with and build a relationship. Over time, if you effectively engage with a top-ranked blogger and develop a working relationship, they will likely talk about your brand, help you tell your story, or do a guest blog post in which they reference your mailing list.

We have found that most companies struggle with thinking of tactics. At Media Connect Partners, this is where we usually get called in to help. We specialize in helping our clients come up with creative tactics for each of their goals, building these tactics out, and helping them deploy them.

After you have listed how to measure success for each goal and tactics for reaching them, it is time to go down one more level and measure all of it to determine the numbers. You need to be able to show: Here is our baseline, here is where we are, here are the tactics we deployed, and here is where we are today. You report all the way up so you can say, "Okay, Mr. Marketing Director, here is our goal, here's what we did, here's how we measured it, and here's the success we had." Over the course of time, you can keep measuring the success you're having in meeting your goals. This is measurable ROI in our book.

What are you measuring? You could be measuring unique website visits, parts of the country you're engaged in, sentiment, followers, interactions (retweets, shares, comments), and so on. There are many things you can measure that are unique to your business. For example, if you run a brick-and-mortar retail establishment, you might track the number of people that say a secret key word when they walk into the store, show your tweet on their smartphone, or something like this. The trick is not getting hung up on what social media can do for you until you identify what your goals are, the measure you will use to make sure you have met the goals, and the tactics you will deploy, including social media.

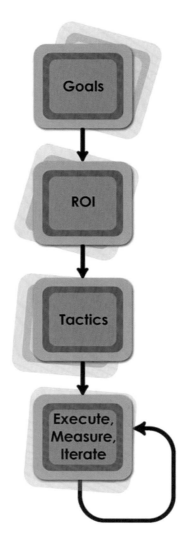

All of this must be measurable for this model to work. So it's full ROI: goals, tactics, and measuring. If you put these in a circle, you can iterate it and do it again. Not every tactic is going to be successful. Some tactics we've tried have been zeros, not heroes. This is why you must measure them and do so correctly, so you know if you've been successful or not.

Key Platforms for Your Social Media Strategy

There are social media platforms you must not overlook when creating your social media strategy. The trend is definitely toward media, so the platforms that allow you to tell your story and share your brand through pictures or video are the ones you do not want to ignore. The names may change, but for now, Instagram, Vine, and YouTube are three platforms you can use to tell your story through photos and video that work extremely well. Your blog is also timeless. (We will have blogs forever, even after this book is in a landfill one day.) When we talk about social media platforms, the blog is really the key, though often overlooked by those seeking the "new thing." In Chapter 7, I talked about the ROR funnel, the importance of driving people down to your website and your blog, so keep in mind, this is a platform you cannot afford to overlook. You may consider Facebook, Twitter, blog, and YouTube your top four platforms, but of the four, your blog is the biggest key to your overall success.

The live event or live webcast is a phenomenal platform. At Media Connect Partners, we produce live, interactive webcasts for brands around the world, and they've been very, very effective with this medium. Imagine a webcast where hundreds or thousands of people can interact with your brand through a spokesperson or personality and one-on-one conversation. The brand can look into the eyes of participating fans or friends and say: "Thank you for your question. Here's why we think our breath mints are better than everybody else's breath mints," or "Here's why we think our school is better than everybody else's," or "I feel your concern. Let's talk about it. Go into the chat room and ask me that question with a little more detail so I can really answer you. I want to make sure we really get to your question."

Inexplicably, too many brands use webcasting like a YouTube channel and talk one way, offering no opportunity for interaction with the audience. The reason our events are successful and our clients say, "That's a great platform," is we employ two-way communication that builds relationships, transparency, and loyalty with fans, friends, followers, and others.

Recently, one of our clients, Oral Roberts University (ORU - @OralRobertsU) in Tulsa, Oklahoma, announced the appointment of a new president, Dr. Billy Wilson. Thousands of alumni all around the world were wondering, "Who is this new president?" So ORU, the smart organization they are, hired us to create a live webcast. This medium enabled our moderator and Dr. Wilson to engage with alumni around the world. We created a landing page and hosted live chat, live Twitter, and live Facebook. Any alum anywhere in the world could interact with us online, ask a question, and get a near real-time response. Dr. Wilson was able to interact with them: "Jim, you're an alum. Great to hear from you today," "What year did you graduate, Sal?" and "I understand your concern, Sarah. Let me talk about that." After the event, alumni were saying: "Wow, that was awesome," "The school really did a great job on this," and "Thanks for engaging us through a medium that makes sense."

Ten years ago, this was not possible. Look how far we've come. Webcasting and live events have given brands an unprecedented capability for building loyalty, transparency, engagement, and most importantly, right relationships with customers and donors, existing donors and prospects, fans, followers, and others. Whether you are a university or a company selling breath mints, it makes no difference. (When I think about it, a breath mint company could have a great webcast on breath issues, give away some free mints, and have some fun with it as well.) The webcast shows you care about your fan base and customers and that you're not just there to talk at people and sell, like a TV commercial.

While clicking through the television channels a few months ago, I came upon a live webcast by a breakfast brand. When I tuned in to it, it was basically just like watching a TV show. They missed a huge opportunity. After all, I can watch a TV show anytime. They missed a golden opportunity to actually engage and interact. They used only a fraction of the potential of the webcast medium.

Establishing a strategy is a lot of work. I am sure this has dawned on you as you've read this chapter. You may be thinking to yourself, *Oh, my goodness, what have we done? How are we ever going to execute all of this?* Trust me—just take it a day at a time, and you can do it. The payoff comes in six, nine, or twelve months, when you see how far you've come, measure your goals, and see the success you've had. That's the payoff. You'll have a smile on your face, and your boss will have a smile on his or hers as well.

As you start building your strategy, grab a baseline—a number: What is your sentiment level today? What are your follower numbers? What is your number of interactions? What is your number indicating your reach into different parts of the world, or country? Build up a strategy, execute it, measure it, and bask in your success. When someone asks you, "Do we have any ROI social media?" you will be able to say, "You bet, and here it is." I've been in business in this space for over five years now, and I've had a chance to see this happen time and time again. It's always exciting.

CHAPTER 9

Maintaining Your Social Media Edge (Keep an Eye on the Periphery)

"A good hockey player plays where the puck is.
A great hockey player plays where the puck is going to be."
—Wayne Gretzky

"If you worry about where everyone else is right now,
you'll always be playing catch-up. Instead, strive for
innovation and stay on the lookout for your next move.
If you aren't in a position to anticipate and be nimble,
determine how you can start changing your organization."
—Brian Murray

Don't get comfortable. Don't get comfortable in social media and digital media. It all moves too quickly. Not long ago, I sat down with a twenty-something young man who works in the social media space for a large Fortune X corporation. I was consulting with their firm on social media strategies. He looked at me and said, "You know, Brian, I really get our demographic for our company."

I said, "Oh yeah? That's great!"

"I really get it...because I'm twenty-five and not old," he said as he looked at me across the table.

This got me thinking. Just because you're in a certain age bracket, it doesn't mean you can communicate with others in that bracket. Nor does it mean you can allow yourself to get lazy in social media, trusting your youthful intuition to carry you, when you truly need to roll with the rapid changes and adapt your approach to succeed.

Social media is an ever-shifting space and moves so quickly that you need to run to keep up with it (at least), to get ahead of it (at best). In this case, the young man I was talking to has the technical experience and the "geek cred" to know quite a few platforms—Instagram, Pinterest, Vine, Quora, Keek, and others—but he didn't have the business acumen to know how to correctly turn them into business tools. As an executive, you want to know what a social media platform can do for your company. You ask, "What does this platform do for our corporate goals and objectives?" You want the people handling your social media to ask these questions before you have to, and to not only understand the functions of the technology, but apply them as business tools that will meet your goals. Don't get comfortable. Make sure those handling your social media stay nimble, knowing the tools they are using today, or the ways they use them may well change six months from now.

The One Constant: Change

In 2012, the Twitter corporation released Vine, a mobile application (app) that enables its users to create and post short video clips. At the time of this writing, it had gained steam rapidly and become quite popular. Two years ago, it didn't exist. It's simple for a corporation like Twitter or Facebook to introduce a new tool which quickly becomes a leader in its space. Were there other video platforms out before Vine? Sure. But Twitter came in as the 800-pound gorilla and made up their own, and now it's a market leader.

Over the past few years we've seen a number of social media platforms come and go. MySpace of course is the poster child for this truth. The popular Foursquare (launched in 2009) once had a competitor called Gowalla (launched in 2007). They came along at a time when a number of geo-aware social media applications were being introduced to the world. Everyone seemed to be in one of the two camps: Gowalla or Foursquare. As it turned out, those who joined the Foursquare camp won out, because in 2012, Gowalla closed its doors after being acquired by Facebook in December, 2011. In the television viewer and media space, GetGlue and Miso are the chief competitors. GetGlue broke through the ranks to become the leader in that space. So in geo-aware social media both Foursquare and Gowalla were there, but then after several years, Foursquare assumed the lead. In the media and television space, there were Miso and GetGlue, but GetGlue assumed the lead. When you invest time and resources in a social platform, you simply never know for sure how successful it is ultimately going to be.

Interestingly, even the mighty Facebook may have some issues. At this writing, I've had three people over the last three weeks tell me the same thing: Their teenagers don't use Facebook anymore because "it's boring," and they've moved on to Instagram. Will Facebook share the fate of Myspace? Time will tell—perhaps sooner than later. Platforms trend. They come and go.

When you build your social media strategy, you may see several different players in the same space. You need to do the research to know which one to align with, and do your best to determine which ones will succeed and which ones will fail. There is always the chance you might choose the wrong one from time to time—in fact, it is almost certain you will. When you do, you have to iterate and change your platforms and strategies to adapt to the new reality.

Get Eyes on the Periphery

The key to knowing what's on the horizon is keeping your eyes on the periphery. Get eyes on what's going on around you so you can remain nimble, deploying to new platforms and tools as they are introduced. To do this, your social media point people should regularly ask knowledgeable friends, better yet, consultants who live social media 24/7, what they see happening, which platforms are gaining in the space, which ones are losing, and where they see the trends happening. It's important for members of your team to spend a portion of each day reading blogs, communicating with influencers, and making sure they stay on top of the trends and technology. You don't want to waste time building strategies for a platform that is not going to exist in six months.

Here are some sources for you and your social media team to bookmark and keep an eye on to track cycles and trends and maintain your edge in the social media space.

News Sources
- Mashable (http://mashable.com/)
- Daily Dot (http://www.dailydot.com/)
- The Verge (http://www.theverge.com/)
- TechCrunch (http://techcrunch.com/
- Buzzfeed (http://www.buzzfeed.com/)
- All Top - Social Media (http://social-media.alltop.com/
- Fast Company (http://www.fastcompany.com/)
- AdAge (http://adage.com/
- US News & World Report: Science & Technology (http://www.usnews.com/usnews/tech/tehome.htm)
- Inc.com (http://www.inc.com/managing-technology)
- Huffington Post: Social Media (http://www.huffingtonpost.com/news/social-media/)
- PR Newswire (http://www.prnewswire.com/)
- Cynopsis (http://www.cynopsis.com/)
- Digiday (http://www.digiday.com/)

Official Social Media Platform Blogs
- Facebook Blog (https://blog.facebook.com/)
- Twitter Blog (http://blog.twitter.com/)
- Google Blog (http://googleblog.blogspot.com/)
- LinkedIn Blog (http://blog.linkedin.com/)

Newsletters
- HubSpot (http://www.hubspot.com/)
- Post Rocket (http://getpostrocket.com/)
- Jon Loomer (http://www.jonloomer.com/)
- Search Engine People Blog (http://www.searchenginepeople.com/blog)
- Media Bistro (http://www.mediabistro.com/)

Other
- Gawker (http://gawker.com/)

Affiliate Marketers
- Mari Smith (http://www.marismith.com/)
- Russell Brunson (http://www.russellbrunson.com/)

Tools
- Crowdbooster (http://crowdbooster.com/)
- Piqora (formerly Pinfluencer) (http://www.piqora.com/)
- PinPuff (http://www.pinpuff.com/)
- Statigr.am (http://statigr.am/)
- Klout (http://klout.com/home)
- PeerIndex (http://www.peerindex.com/)
- EmpireAvenue (http://www.peerindex.com/)
- Sprout Social (http://sproutsocial.com/)
- Trendrr (http://trendrr.com/tv/)

- TweetStats (http://www.tweetstats.com/)
- Simply Measured (http://simplymeasured.com/)

I believe that social media reinvents itself every four to six months. So the goals you set on January 1 and the tactics you use to support them (as we mentioned in Chapter 7) need to be revisited June 1 (if not before). To keep your social media marketing plan effective, you must revisit and revise it every few months and make changes as needed—iterate. Iteration is a great tool. See the graphic above. The ability to iterate, to periodically refine your social media strategy, building on what is working, ditching what isn't, and incorporating promising new tools and platforms, is a vitally important key to your success in social media marketing. This is a sound business practice and a vital social media marketing tactic.

Know Your Limits

If you've learned anything in this book, you've discovered it takes intentional thought, careful planning, a good chunk of time, ongoing research to keep up with what's happening, looking to the future, and strong business acumen to implement and manage a successful social media plan. Maintaining your social media edge simply takes time. Hiring a part-time intern to spend thirty minutes a day managing your social presence before a global audience just isn't going to cut it. I guarantee you won't be successful.

Not long ago, I was at the Genius Bar of my local Apple store getting my MacBook Pro looked at by a genius. The genius helping me asked, "What do you do?"

"I own a social media agency," I said.

Next to me was a man getting his Mac fixed. He said, "What's that? What did you say you do?"

"I own a social media agency," I repeated.

@brianboyd

"We have to talk. I own a company and we don't know what we're doing with social media. We've been looking for somebody like you," he said as he handed me his card. "Let's have a conversation."

"You bet, anytime," I said.

Here was the CEO of a company who recognized he needed to use social media. He didn't have the resources to do this in-house, and he knew it. And he knew better than to run to the local college and grab the first twenty-something he could find to "manage" his social. As luck would have it, we were sitting next to each other at a Genius Bar. Ideally, as a CEO you know what you've got in-house...and you know what you don't. Surround yourself with smart people, as you already do in other areas. Look to them to help bring social media success to your organization.

Signs of a Sinking Platform

If you're measuring and monitoring your ROI and ROR on a regular basis, you'll notice undulations. If you see interactions drop, referrals dip, or engagement falling, these are signs that something is wrong. Something is not working. If you are part of a blog or a forum and people stop congregating there, it's a sign that it's losing steam. Listening and looking is not an exact science, but you as a brand must know if you are no longer where the people are. The easy measurement is if there is a lack of interaction, a lack of engagement, and the metrics you're measuring aren't there. These may indicate it's time to move out of a platform. If a platform is no longer working for you, shut it down.

When you decide you're not going to use a platform anymore, it is important that you shut it down. You don't want to leave a ghost presence online. We always recommend that a brand actually close the doors on platforms they've shut down. Sometimes they leave a "We've moved!" message there, so people know to go find them elsewhere. For example, if you read my wife's Twitter handle @FranBoyd, it says: "I've moved. I'm now @FranPaceBoyd." She changed her handle to include her maiden name. Still, in most cases, the best idea, depending on the platform, is to actually close it down so people don't see anything there. This way they show up and wonder what's going on, and you risk negative exposure.

Social Media and Your Personal Brand

Social media is not just for corporations, it's for individuals as well. The tools we've talked about in this book and the steps we've walked you through to build your organization's social media initiatives can easily be adapted to you as an individual, as an executive—100 percent. So after you've handed a copy of this book to your marketing team and said, "Make sure you execute on this," think about yourself and how you, as an executive and business leader, can apply these tools to build your own personal brand and meet your goals. The one constant is change and you never know where life leads, though it may well lie beyond your current company.

When people vet you out online, you want them to find exactly what *you* want them to find about you as a person, a father, a mother, an executive, an individual, a business leader, a philanthropist, a nonprofit leader, and so on. Do you want to be in control of this, or do you want others to be in control of it? Do you want to ensure that what's being said about your company and your brand is what comes from you? If so, your personal branding via social media is your opportunity to be in control of what's being said about your brand, your company, and you as a person. I can say from experience, I've been hired based on my own brand that I've put out there, so I know it works and how important it is. You and your company will be hired or see opportunities because of what is written about you online.

Epilogue

I'd love to hear from you. If you've read this book and have additional questions or thoughts—or if you disagree with me ☺—reach out to me on Twitter: @BrianBoyd. You can also find me at brian@mediaconnectpartners.com.

Let's build some ROR together!